lemon poppy seed

MULTITASKING CREATIVITY

PHILIPPE JARRIGEON
Pieds de Poule/
Cochon

Page 7
Pieds de Poule/
Tapisserie

MARTIN NICOLAUSSON
Color

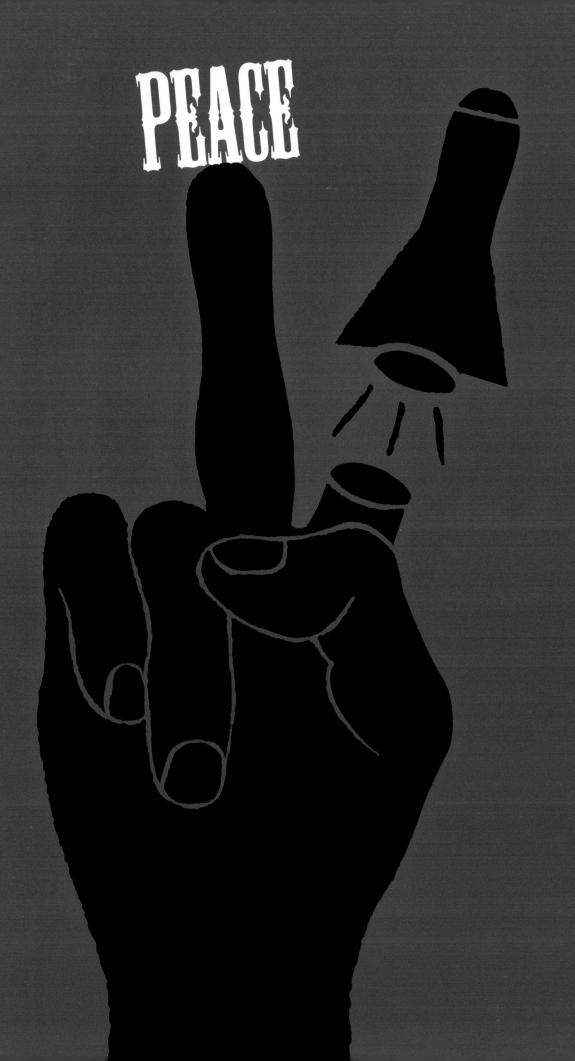

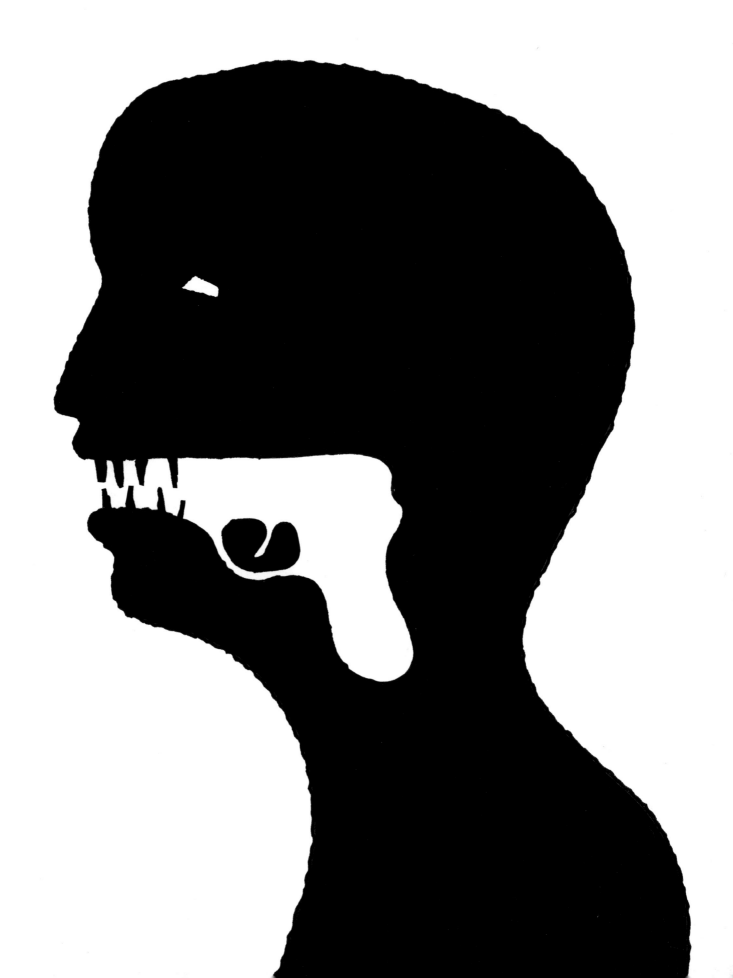

LA MAISON DE BERNARDA ALBA

MISE EN SCÈNE JACQUES NICHET

THÉÂTRE DES 13 VENTS

MONTPELLIER

GARCÍA LORCA

06. 01/ 12. 02 20 07

LA MAISON DE BERNARDA ALBA

06.
01
/12.
02
20
07

THÉÂTRE DES 13 VENTS. MONTPELLIER

GARCÍA LORCA

MISE EN SCÈNE JACQUES NICHET

La FRANCE est à NOUS

THE next MOVE-MENT — Bâtir l'âme d'un pays, le rendre plus entreprenant, plus innovant, plus optimiste, plus simple et funky, c'est le devoir quotidien de chaque citoyen vivant sur le sol français.

NON au NON systématique

THE next MOVE-MENT — C'est un fait, les français ne sont jamais contents. Il est légitime, et très sain, qu'une société s'exprime et revendique ses droits mais on doit lutter contre ce négativisme forcené qui pourrit notre pays.

+de HIP +de HOP

THE next MOVE-MENT — La culture française a pris une nouvelle tournure, les mouvements de pensée prennent vie dans la rue. Ceux qu'on traite de lascars sont en fait nos poètes, trop longtemps évincés par les philosophes stupides.

BLACK BLANC BEUR C'EST ÇA NOS VALEURS

THE next MOVE-MENT — Le paysage français est métissé, exotique, finement sucré. Ce cocktail acidulé de diversités sociales, mentales et culturelles n'est pas un fardeau mais une fierté. Il fonde les valeurs de notre état d'esprit.

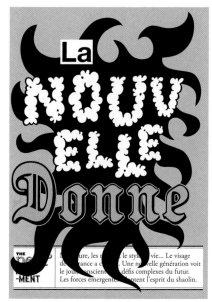

La NOUVELLE Donne

THE next MOVE-MENT — ...ure, les ... le style ... vie... Le visage de ...rance a ... Une nouvelle génération voit le jou... conscien... défis complexes du futur. Les forces émergentes ...ptent l'esprit du shaolin.

2007 Kids Attack

Ninja Power.

THE next MOVE-MENT — Tel le ninja en action, la jeunesse de France brise les vieux mythes, les préjugés, les idées figées et insufle une griffe résolument contemporaine. Les kids dégainent leur style et ça va faire mal.

L'énergie de L'UN-ION

THE next MOVE-MENT — La fusion cosmique des forces émergentes génère une énergie tri-dimensionnelle. Les conservateurs et les bien-pensants sont pris à contre-pied. Les pensées fertiles diffusent un état d'esprit libre.

CES URE

THE next MOVE-MENT — Le mouvement s'empare du territoire de France. Les indécis et les négativistes sont balayés tels de petits Ewoks. Les concepts miteux partent en fumée. L'esprit du shaolin impose son flow.

THE next MOVE-MENT — Tel le papillon, le mouvement d'après, celui du renouveau, déploie sa philosophie et ouvre la voie d'une France libre et décontractée. L'amour, l'harmonie et la créativité sont les nouvelles bases.

2

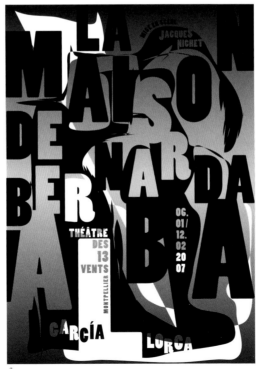

3

À 2 C'EST MIEUX
¹ *The Next Movement*
² *The Next Movement*
  in the Streets of Paris
³ *Bernarda Alba*

HERMAN MELVILLE

MACBETH

William Shakespeare

SACRED MTN.
Njet

VICTOR MELAMED
[1] _Terminator_
[2-3] _Illustrations for a Short
Story by Neil Gaiman_

At One in the Sun

I AM MINT CONDITION
At One in the Sun

Page 23
SACRED MTN.
Forest Cooker
of Breakfast

1

2

MUSEUM STUDIO
[1] *The Magic Poster*
[2] *Ceremony Mask*

Page 25
KOLEKTIV
Norwegian Dream

ALEXANDER EGGER
Satellites Mistaken
for Stars

OOSE A BRIGHT MORNING

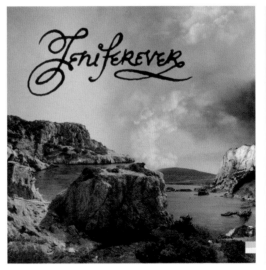
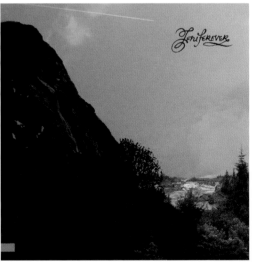

HIJACKYOURLIFE
Choose a Bright Morning

JULIEN PACAUD
Polaroids That Never
Existed

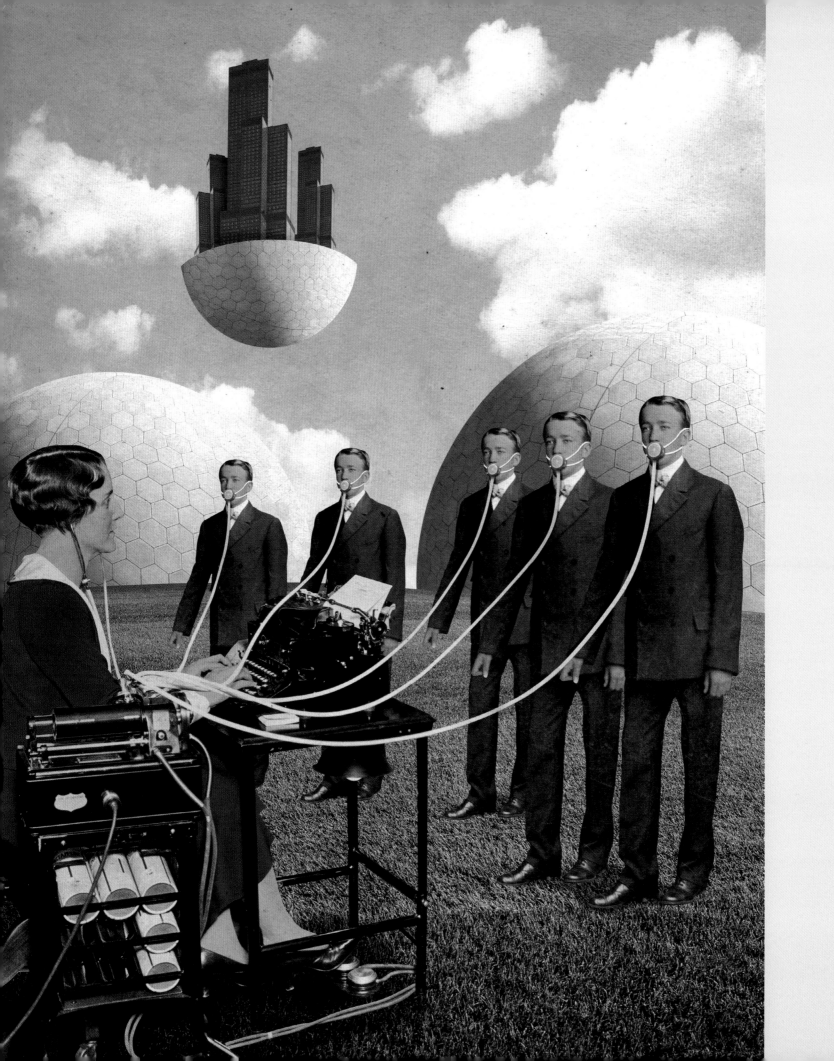

JULIEN PACAUD
Monsieur Mystère

EMMANUEL POLANCO
Tarot of Marseille:
The Moon

Page 36
Tarot of Marseille:
The Star

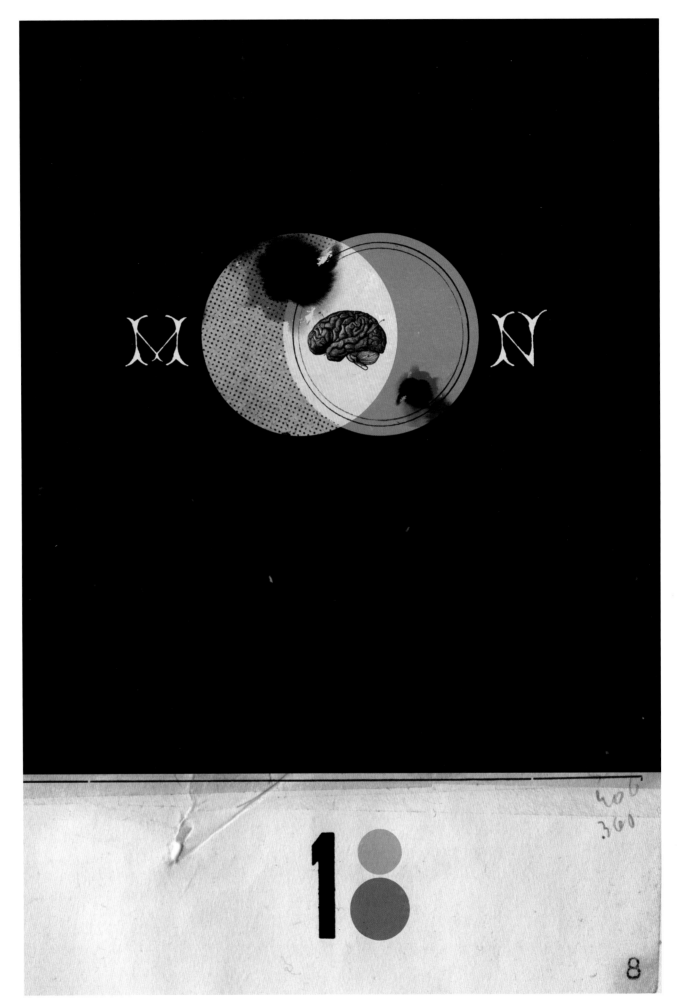

Luddites of the world unite and take over.

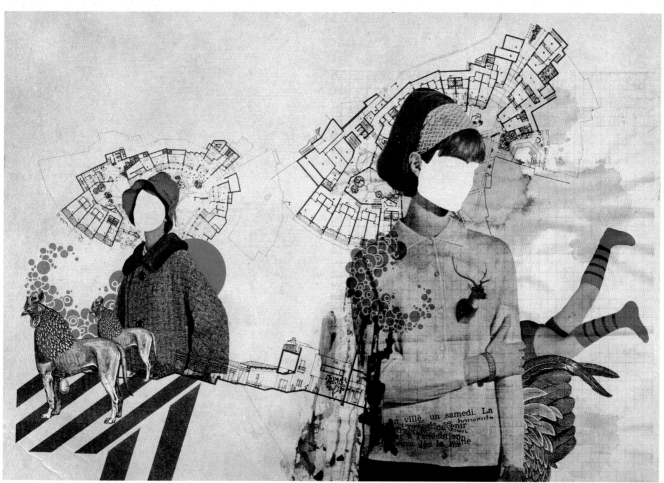

JULIEN PACAUD
[1] *Memories of Tomorrow*
[4] *World Construction Kit*

SEBASTIEN LYKY
[2] *Break*

EMMANUEL POLANCO
[3] *Tarot of Marseille:*
   The Lovers

FRIDAY 12·29
Building
Better
Bombs
@Big V's

with
Assassinations, Ladyslipper, Shoeshiners

www.onefootinfront.com

45

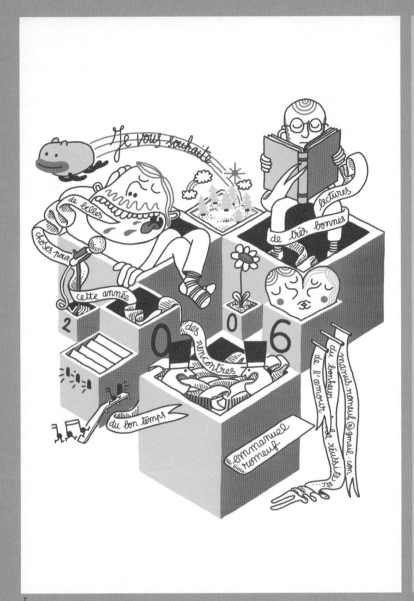

EMMANUEL ROMEUF
[1] *Welcome Lyon*
[2] *Best Wishes 2006*
[3] *Fêtes de Bayonne 2007/*
  Bayonne's Feria 2007

ne pas s'arrêter de pomper!

MA~
[1] *Nouveau Casino*
   Décembre 2006
[2] *Nouveau Casino*
   Novembre 2006
[3] *Nouveau Casino*
   Octobre 2006

EMILY FORGOT
Wishing Cards

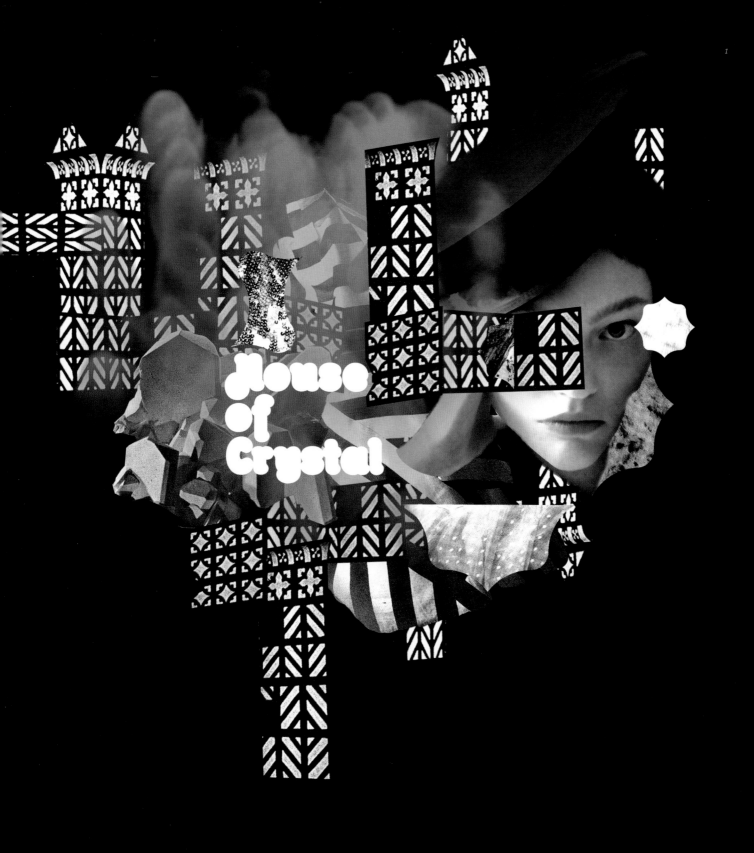

House
of
Crystal

2

3

FOLKERT DE JONG JAMES COHAN GALLERY LES SALTIM-BANQUES

Opening:
Saturday October 20,
6-8 pm

James Cohan Gallery

OCTOBER 20 – NOVEMBER 24, 2007

Folkert de Jong
LES SALTIMBANQUES

1

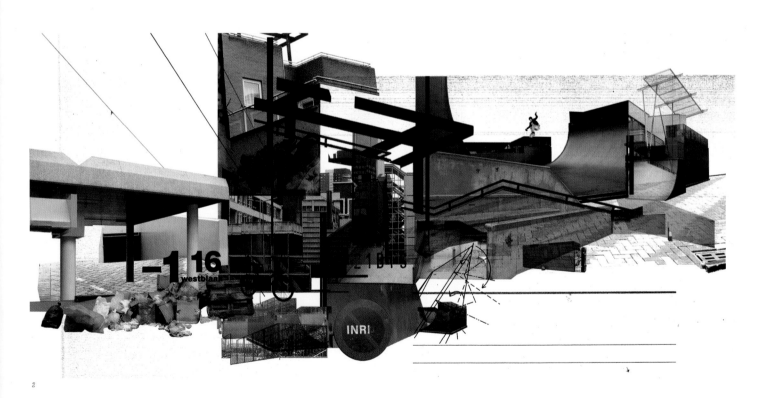

2

21BIS
[1] *Rotterdam*
   Station Blaak
[2] *Rotterdam*
   West Blaak

Page 63
Project 360°

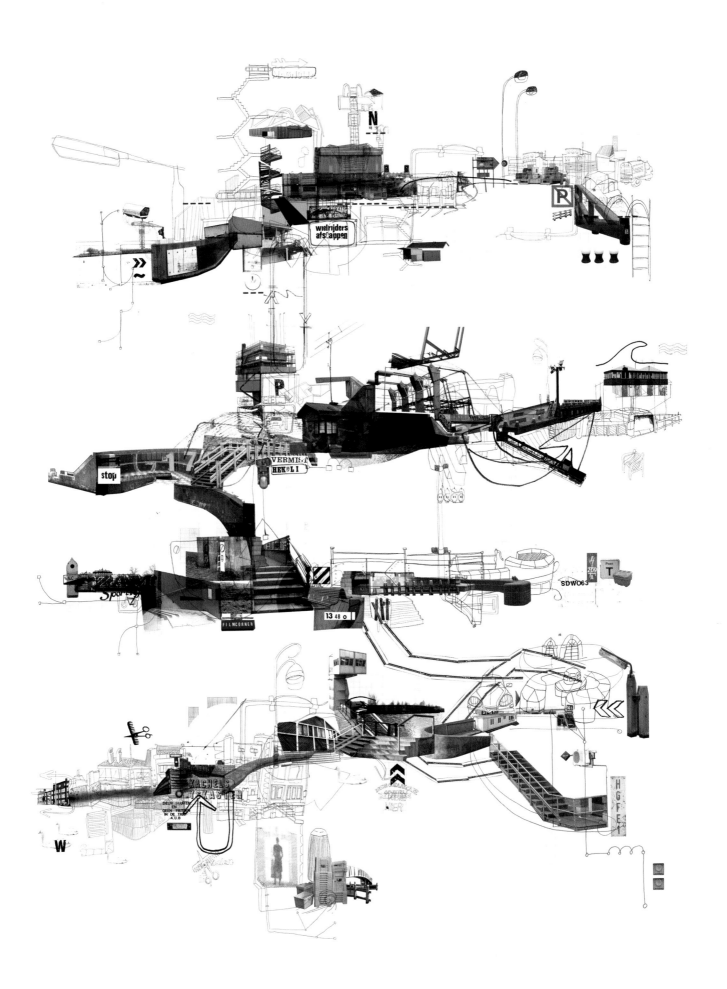

21BIS
Untitled

Page 65
FONS SCHIEDON
University of Twente
(Compilation)

64

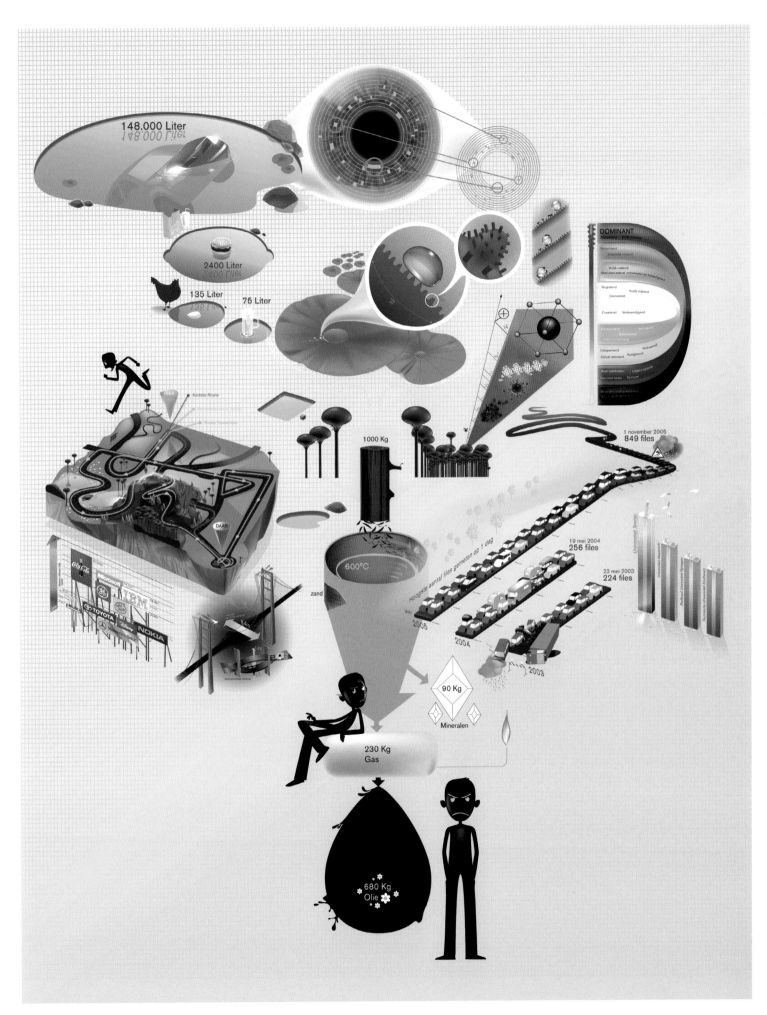

ALL SIGNS POINT TO YES.

KATHRYN MACNAUGHTON
All Signs Point to Yes

Page 66
Posies

MATT W. MOORE
East Coast
Page 76
Progress

CODY HOYT
You Never Know...

Page 78
Big Pink

POP PROPAGANDA

COLOR

ALEXANDER EGGER
Flags Disturb
the Atmosphere

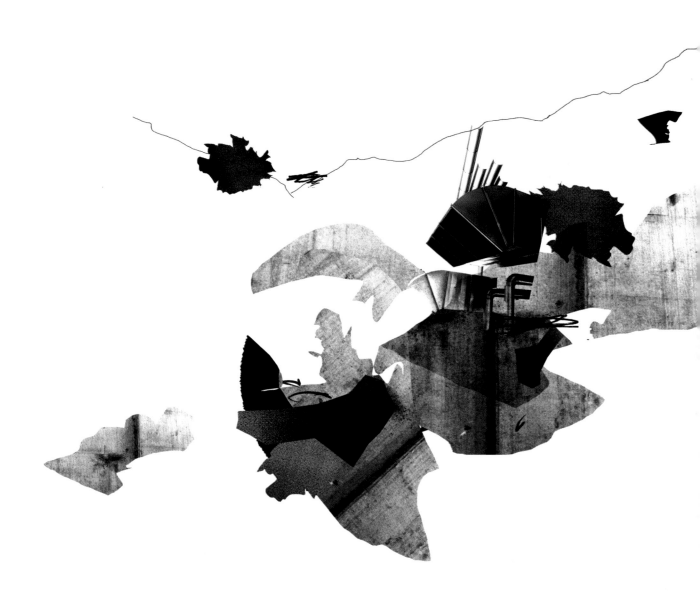

1

2

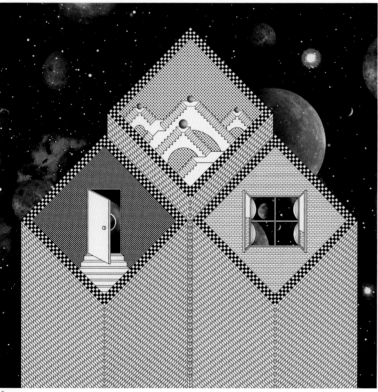

3

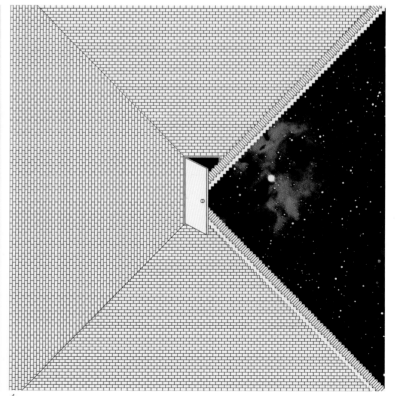

4

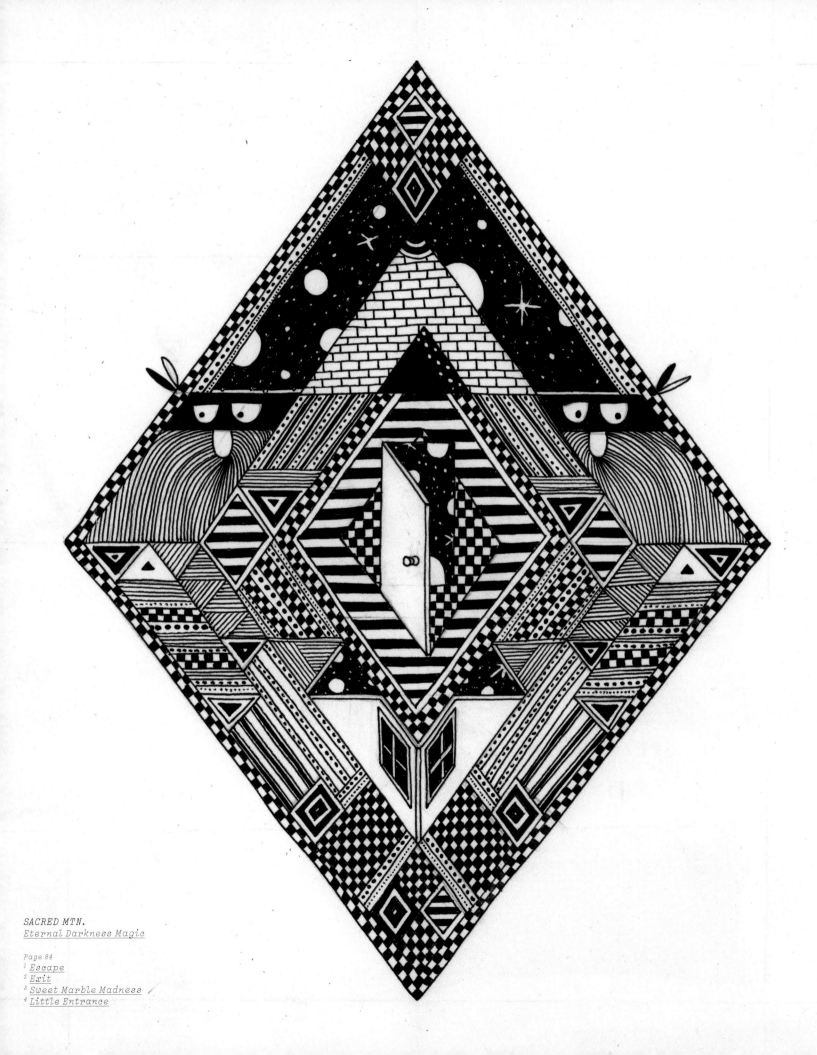

SACRED MTN.
Eternal Darkness Magic

Page 84
[1] Escape
[2] Exit
[3] Sweet Marble Madness
[4] Little Entrance

LULA
Pappervik

EMMANUEL POLANCO
[1] *Camus, l'Absurde*
[2] *Camus, la Révolte*
[3] *Albert Camus*

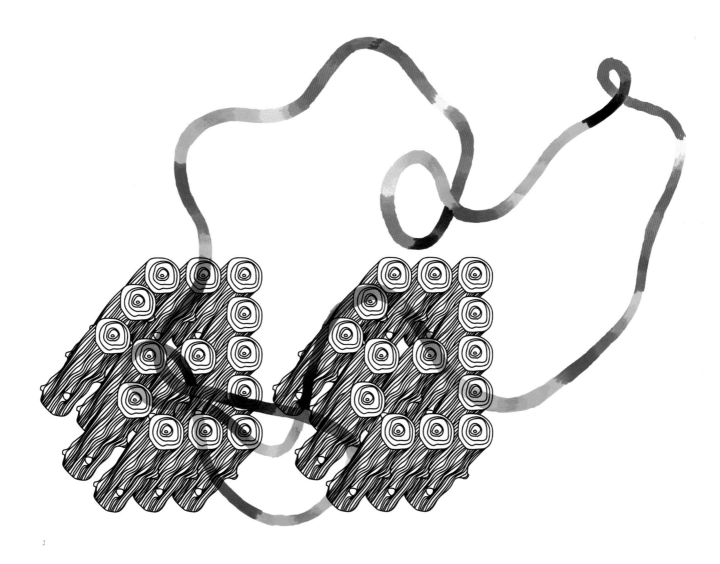

1

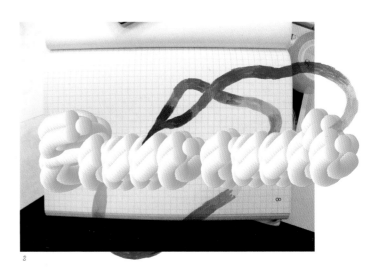

2

NATHALIE NYSTAD
Stress

CODY HOYT
Untitled

奇妙で、同等です。

捨て札をセットすることで多少の基本的な心の数学が助けます。手を半端な番号を付けられていさえしたタイルに分けてください。10
の倍数は偶数で、そのような数の法律はそれを私たちに話します：−(均衡がとれて、+均衡がとれて、+均衡がとれる) 10(奇妙であるこ
と+奇妙であること+同等であること)の同等の可能な倍数=10同等の可能な倍数か(半端で、+半端である、+半端な)= 奇妙である あ
るいは （同等で、+同等で、+奇妙で)=奇妙である。もし手が5枚の半端な番号を付けられたタイルを持っていれば、あなたは捨てること
ができません。もしあなたの手が4枚の半端な番号を付けられたタイルを持っていれば、同等の番号を付けられたタイルから始めることに
よって捨て札を捜して、他の2つをそれに加えてください。もしあなたの手が3枚の半端な番号を付けられたタイルを持っていれば、(半端
で、+半端である、+同等の)組み合わせの捨て札を捜してください。もしあなたの手が2枚の半端な番号を付けられたタイルを持ってい
れば、それらとの捨て札と同等の番号を付けられたタイルの1枚を捜してください。のために3枚の同等の番号を付けられたタイルへの一瞥
あなたの手が1枚の半端な番号を付けられたタイルを持っている そしてそれをひっくり返すように変えて、捨て札を捜す 残りの4で、あ
なたの手が半端な番号を付けられたタイルを持っていない そして残りの5枚のタイルの捨て札を捜す。

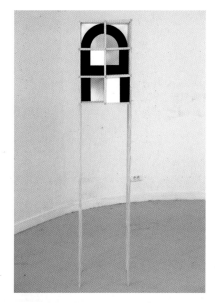
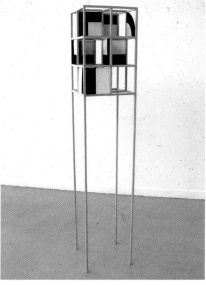
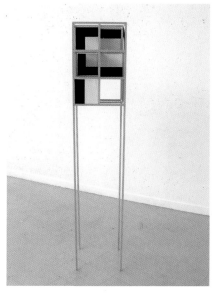

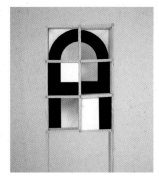

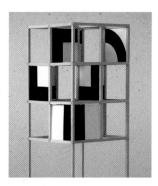
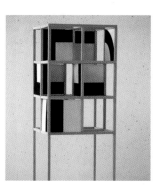

THINK EXPERIMENTAL
Polygraph

Page 97
MEDIUM
House Numbers

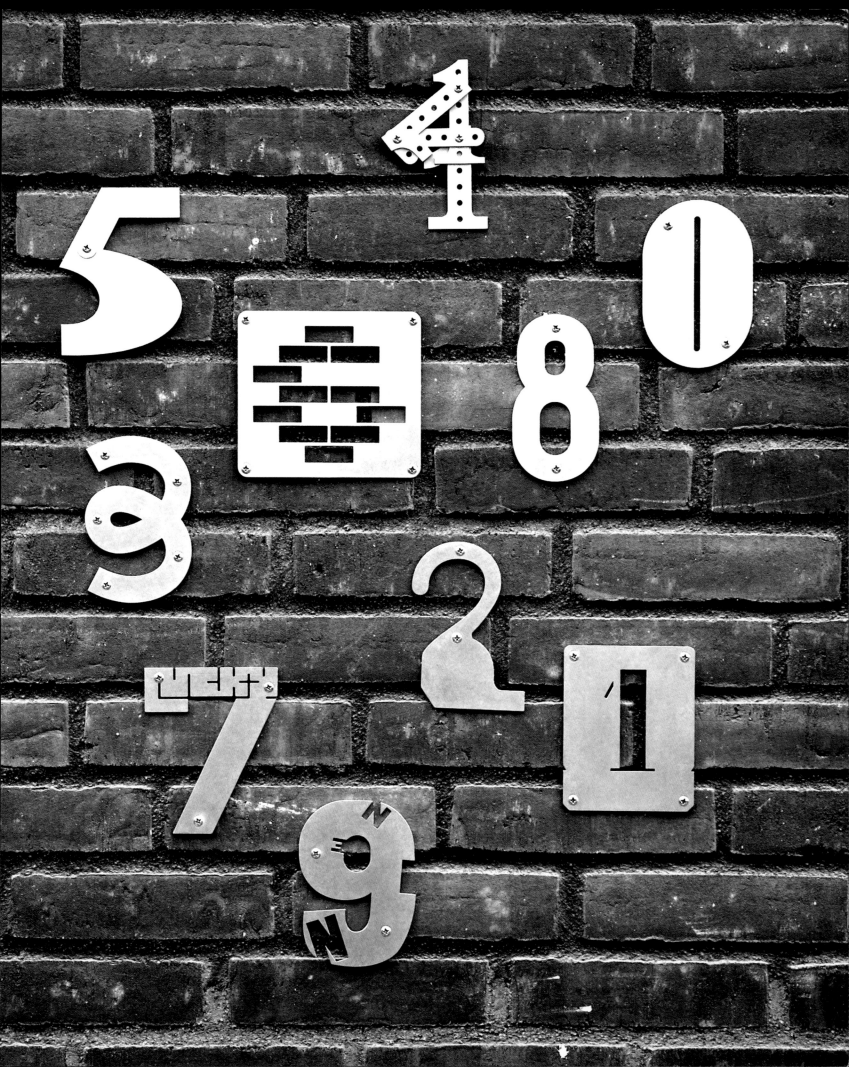

LISA RIENERMANN
Type the Sky

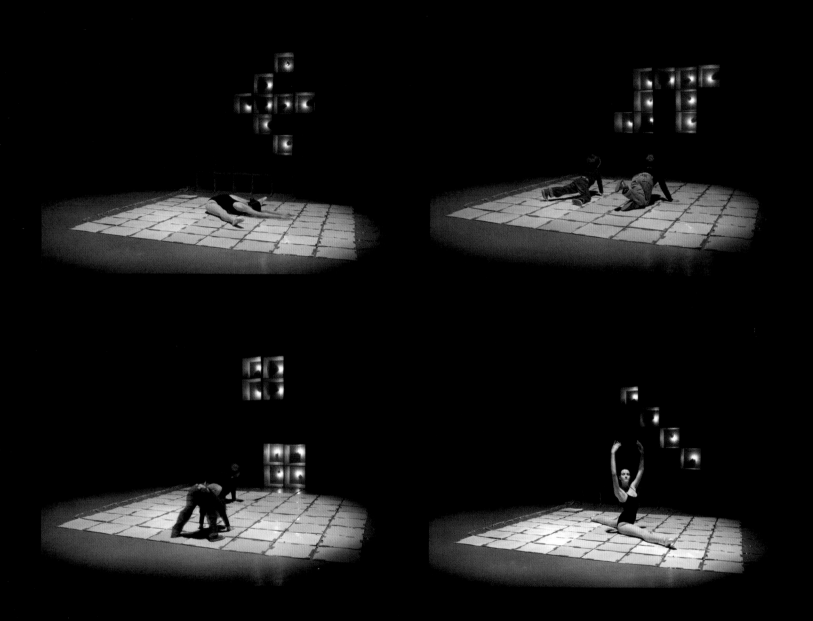

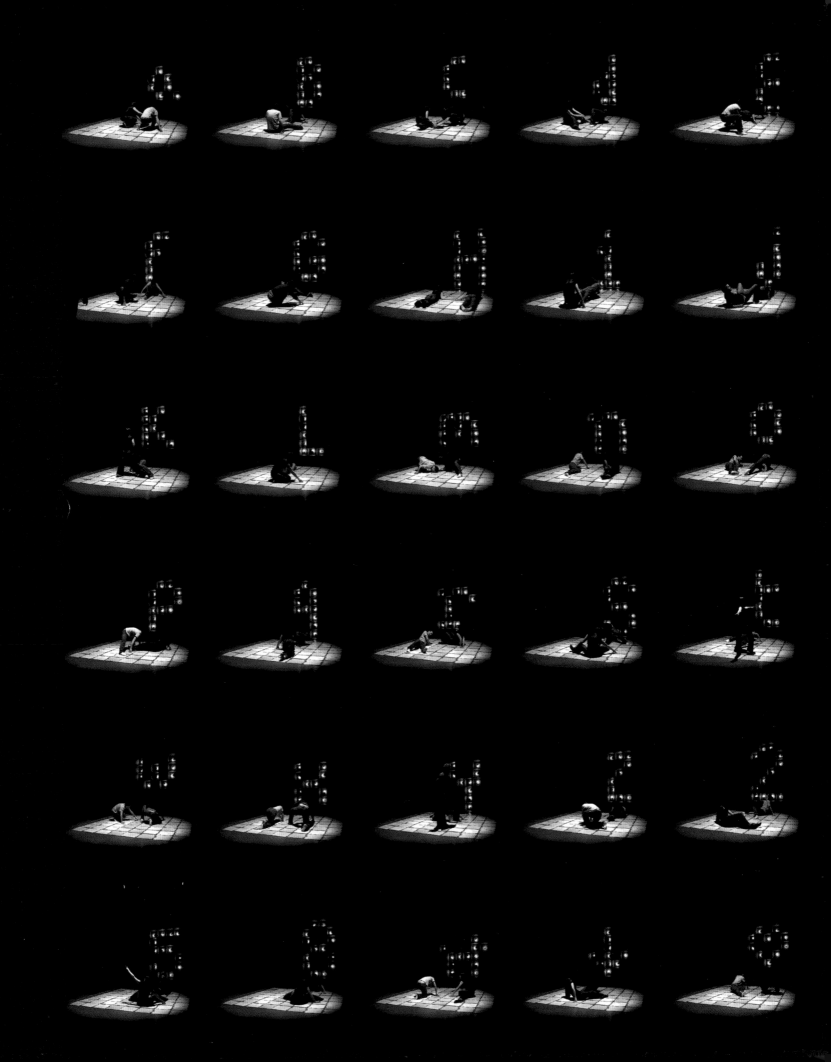

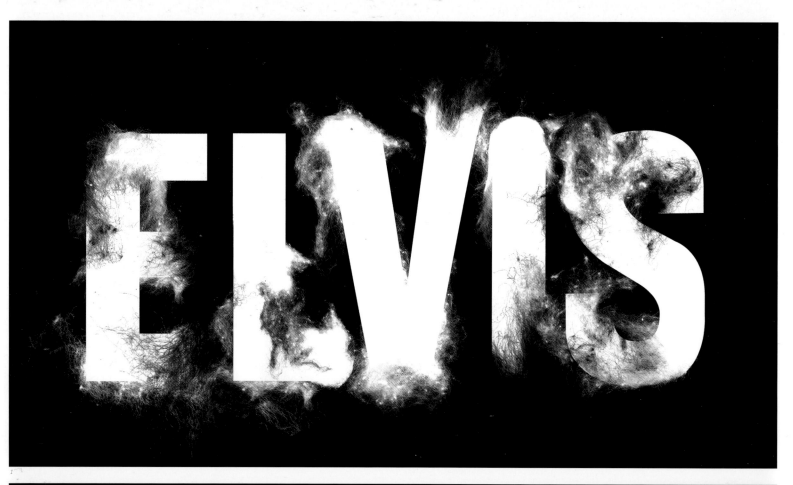

FIVE GET
YEARS PHYSICAL

21.04.2007 EINZELKIND
ZÜRICH M.A.N.D.Y
ROHSTOFFLAGER BOOKA SHADE

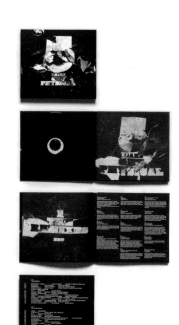

HORT
5 Years
Get Physical Music

SARA HARAIGUE
1-2-3 *Scratch Poster Serie*
4 *Pink*
5 *Black*

1

2

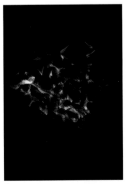

3

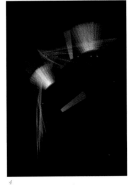

4

5

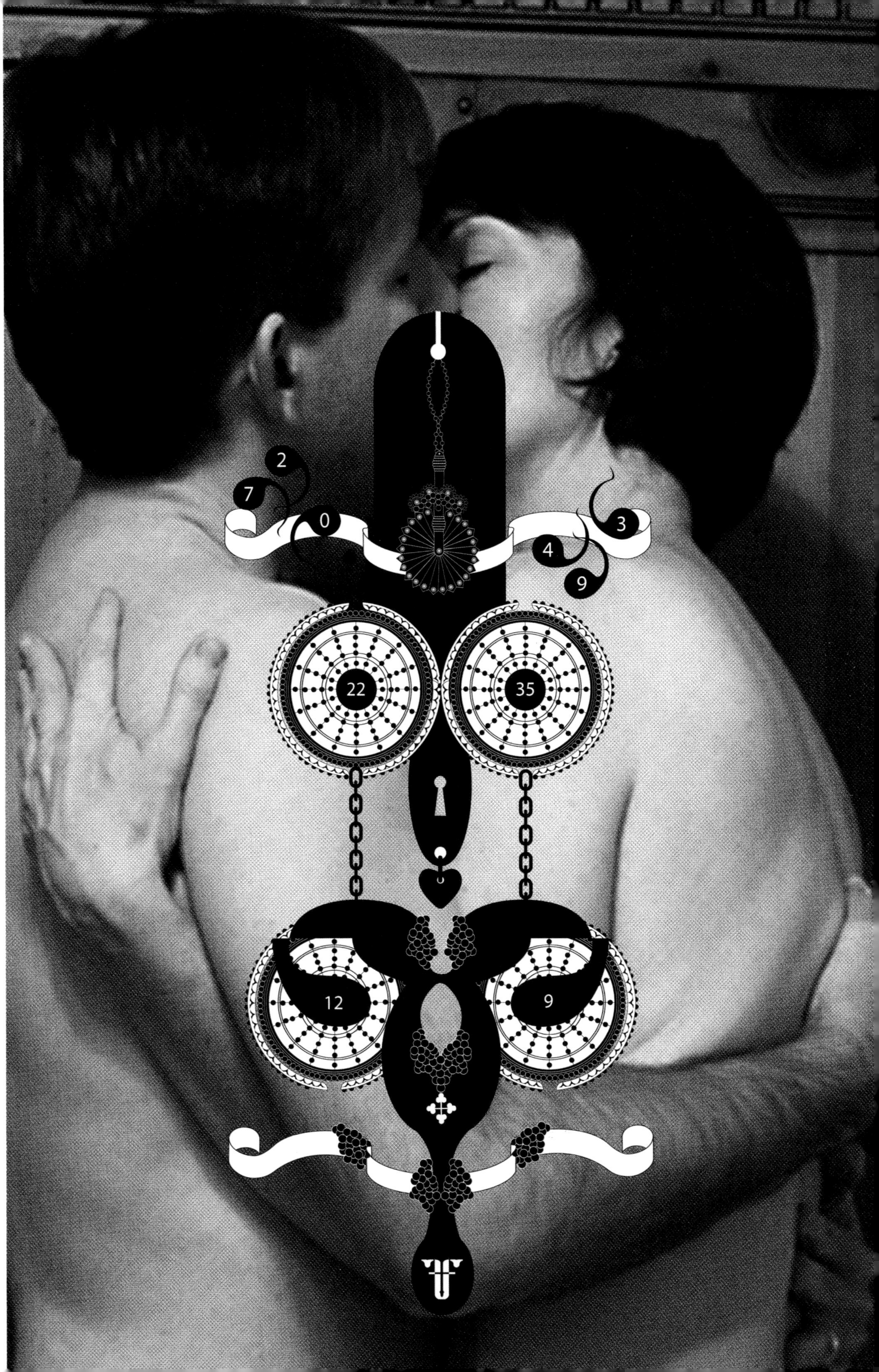
2
7
0
3
4
9
22
35
12
9

1

2

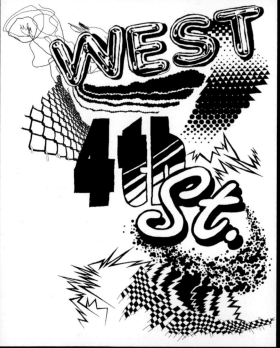

NEVER EFFECT
Untitled

1

2

DAVID CARVALHO
1 *Blind Peony*
2 *Japanese Wedding*

Page 115
Falling in Love

KARPA

恋

1

2

3

4

OPHELIA CHONG
[1] CSS 1
[2] 000 #3
[3] CSS 2
[4] 000 #2

1

OPHELIA CHONG
1 *FrankenSewn*
2 *What He Lost*
3 *The Sound of Clicking*

2

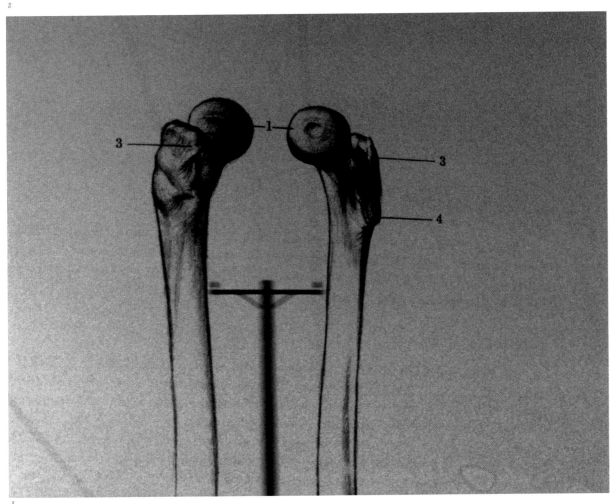

3

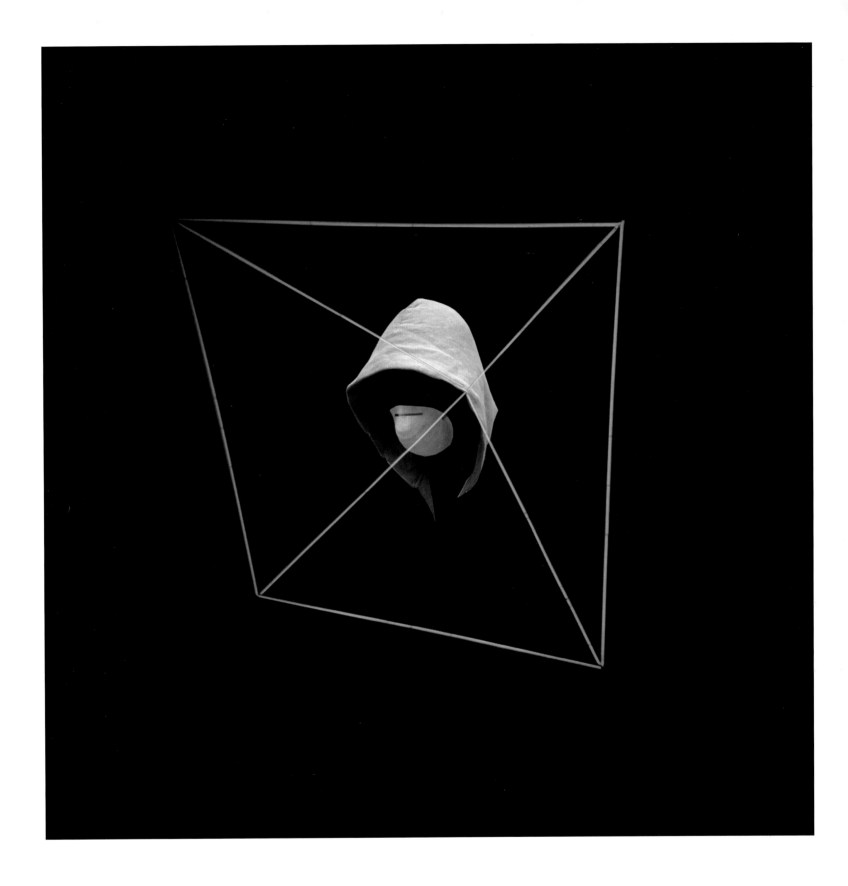

TROY WILLIAMS
Hospital

move along,
nothing to see
here.

HIJACKYOURLIFE
Most Tall Snake

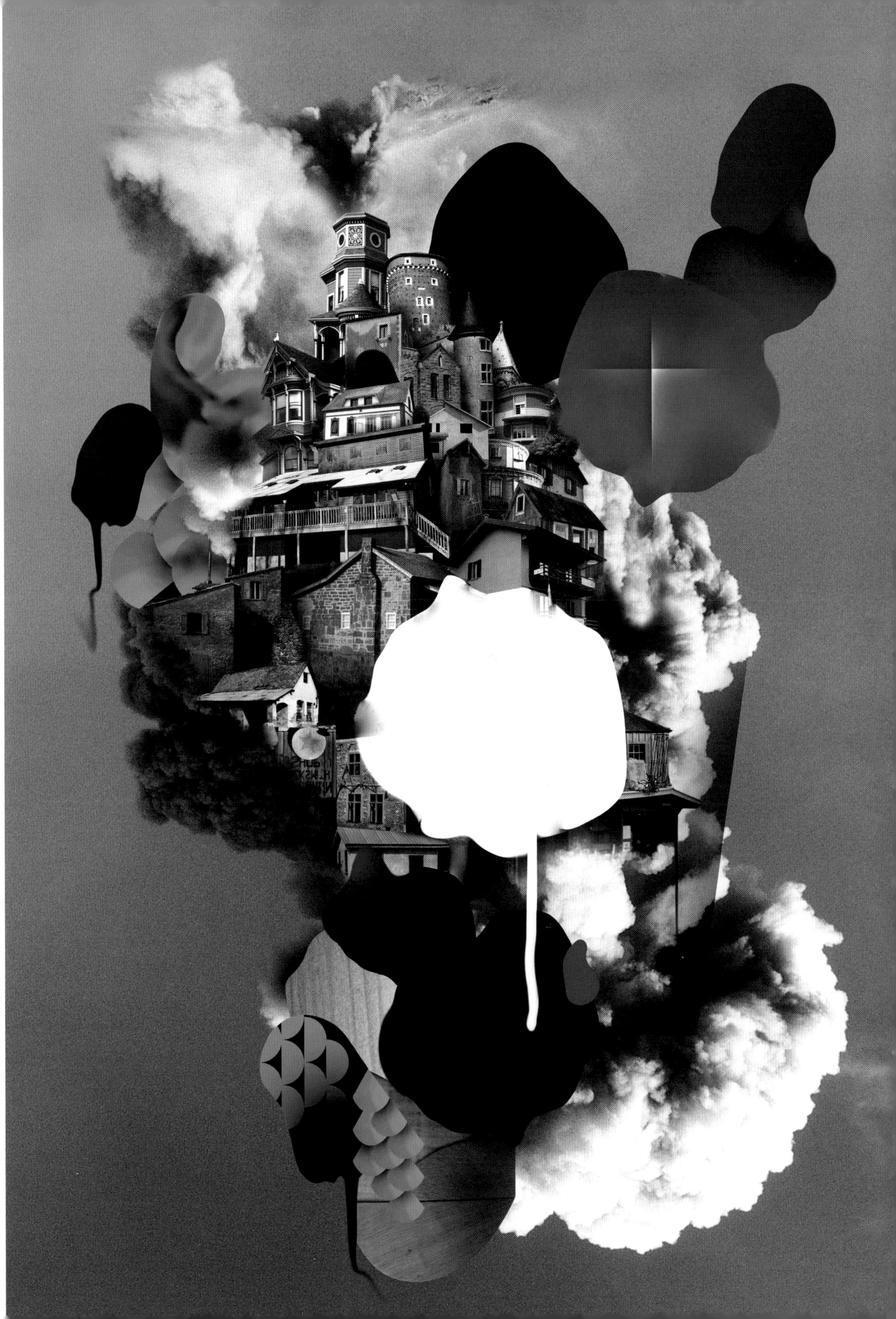

OPHELIA CHONG
1 *Abandoned/I Can't Look
  After You*
2 *Double Espresso*
3 *Sazaah Pyaar Ki*
4 *Amoeba*
5 *Wrath*

Page 131
Living

RAZ OHARA
&
THE ODD
ORCHESTRA

Album
out now!
GPMCD019

playing
LIVE

Get Physical Music
Milastr. 2
10437 Berlin
Germany
Fon +49 (0) 30 440 3328 10

GPMLP019
LC 13285
P&C 2008
Get Physical Music
Made in EU

www.physical-music.com

SIDE A
HAPPY SONG
KISSES
ONE
FRAGMENT
AGONY
THE CASE

SIDE B
WHERE HE AT
COUNTING DAYS
WONDERING
LOVE FOR MRS. RHODES
SET ON YOU

RAZ OHARA AND THE ODD ORCHESTRA

HORT
Raz Ohara and
the Odd Orchestra
(album/single)

le grand
sommeil
pose
le tout

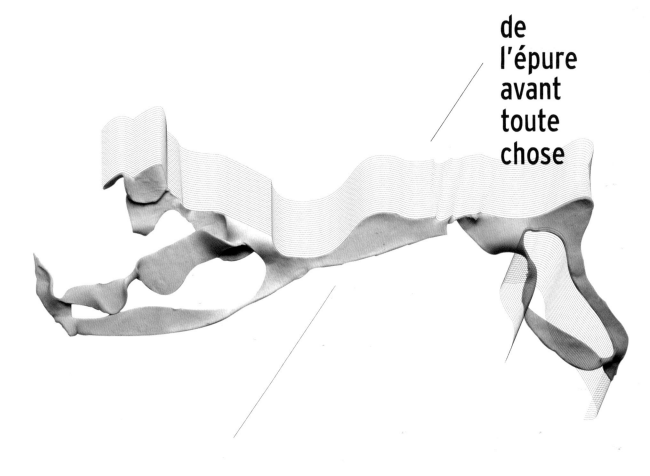

de
l'épure
avant
toute
chose

À 2 C'EST MIEUX
Untitled

Page 136
MIKIS RAOUL
70's Indian

THE LOVE PYRAMID

"WE GOT STONED INSTEAD"

STEVEN HARRINGTON
When John Met Nonny

Page 138
The (Somehow, We Got
Stoned Instead) Pyramid

STEVEN HARRINGTON
Our Pack

Page 141
MEJDEJ
Arvikafestivalen/
Arvika Festival

12 - 14 JULI

ARVIKAFESTIVALEN 08

LIVE THE MUSIC! SCISSOR SISTERS (US) BLOC PARTY (UK) INFECTED MUSHROOM (ISR) IN FLAMES (SE) THE MAGIC NUMBERS (UK) FRONT LINE ASSEMBLY (CAN) HOCICO (MEX) THE ARK (SE) TIMBUKTU (SE) WITHIN TEMPTATION (NL) VNV NATION (UK) HOT CHIP (UK) SLAGSMÅLSKLUBBEN (SE) PAIN (SE) MARIT BERGMAN (SE) MATES OF STATE (US) APOPTYGMA BERZERK (NO) MANDO DIAO (SE) ZEIGEIST (SE) PATRICK WOLF (UK) MELODY CLUB (SE) PORTION CONTROL (UK) SHOUT OUT LOUDS (SE) I AM X (UK) NOUVELLE VAGUE (FR) DARK TRANQUILLITY (SE) MUSTASCH (SE) VAPNET (SE) STRIP MUSIC (SE) SHINY TOY GUNS (US) KRISTIAN ANTTILA (SE) ASHA ALI (SE) MAIA HIRASAWA (SE) SVENSKA AKADEMIEN (SE) TINGSEK (SE) NECRO FACILITY (SE) JUVELEN (SE) WENDY MCNEILL (CAN) KEEP OF KALESSIN (NO) 120 DAYS (NO) HEY WILLPOWER (US) NINE (SE) CONSEQUENCES (SE) EMMON (SE) PLUXUS (SE) FROZEN PLASMA (UK) MISS LI (SE) HANS APPELQVIST (SE) IAMBIA (GR) SABATON (SE) FAMILJEN (SE) EMIL JENSEN (SE) HELLSONGS (SE) KLOQ (UK) DETEKTIVBYRÅN (SE) MIXTAPES & CELLMATES (SE) IDA MARIA (NO) LILLASYSTER (SE) BACKLASH (SE) PAPER FACES (SE) AERIAL (SE) MEMFIS (SE) ASHBURY HEIGHTS (SE) THE MELLOW BRIGHT BAND (SE)

BETALA 100 KR EXTRA OCH VI DONERAR 10st TRÄD TILL NAMIBIA. KÄRLEK TILL SKOGEN! WWW.ARVIKAFESTIVALEN.SE

ARVIKAFESTIVALEN 08

you

&

I

STEVEN HARRINGTON
You & I

Page 142
MIKE PERRY
The Universe at Its Best

SERIPOP
[1] *Extreme Warrior*
[2] *Dramarama*

MIKE PERRY
Purple Waves

MP 2007

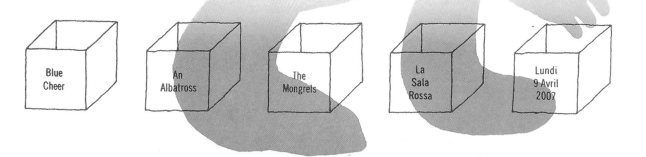

THINK EXPERIMENTAL
Untitled

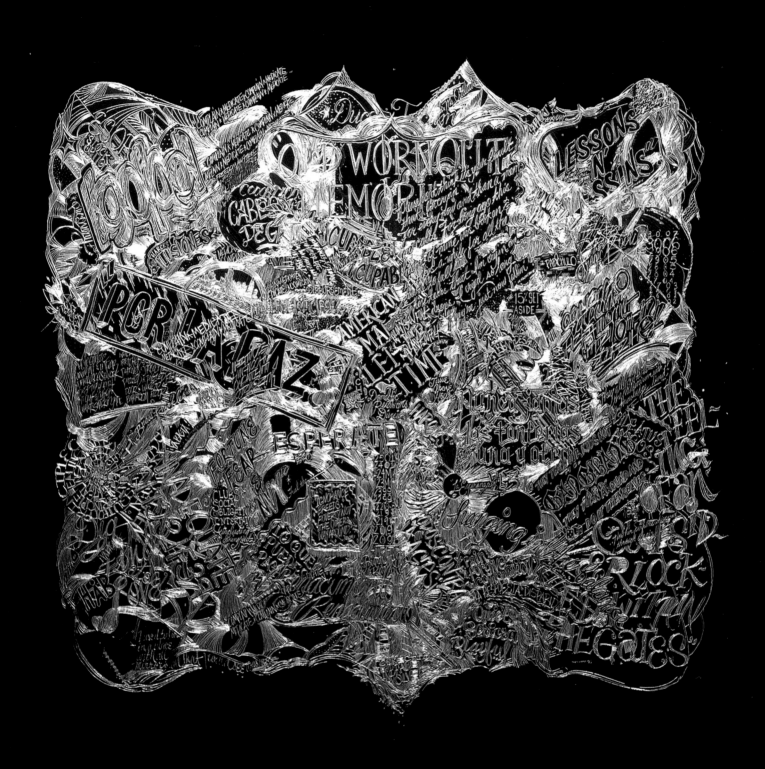

MICHAEL GENOVESE
Untitled

MIKE PERRY
Optical 04

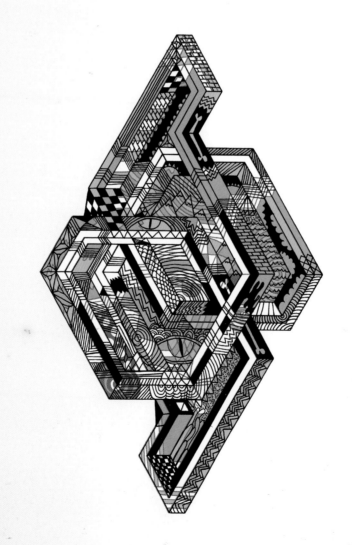

Optical 01

VASCOLO
*Miranda, That Ghost
Isn't Holy Anymore*

THINK EXPERIMENTAL
Untitled

SHOTOPOP
Bear Pukes Toxic Waste
Turns Into Butterflies
Makes Other Bear Happy!

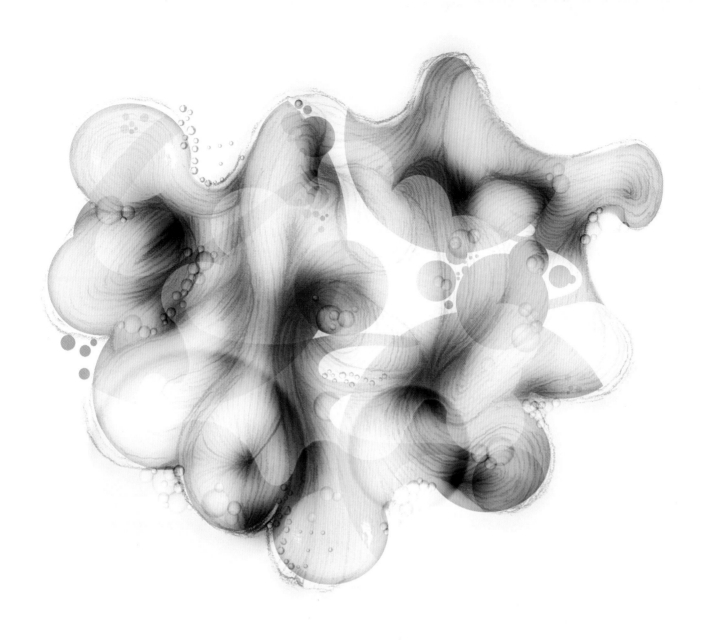

SHOTOPOP
Bubble Island

MARCONI
Black and White

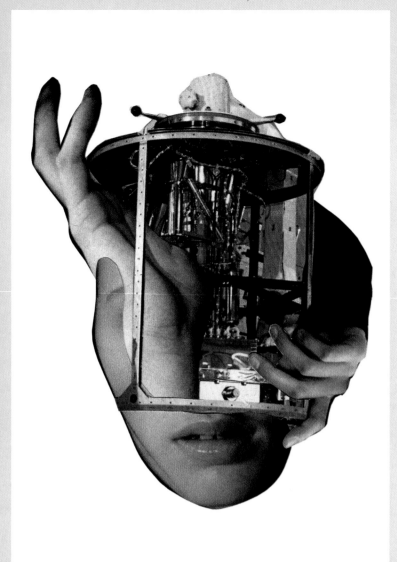

HORT
Corporate & Store
Design/Hayashi

Page 168
BELA BORSODI
Foot Fetish

Page 169
Delikatessen

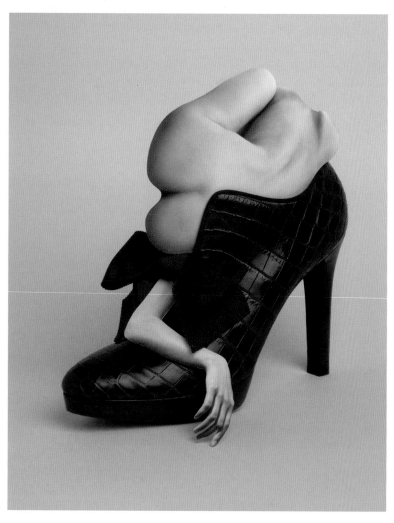

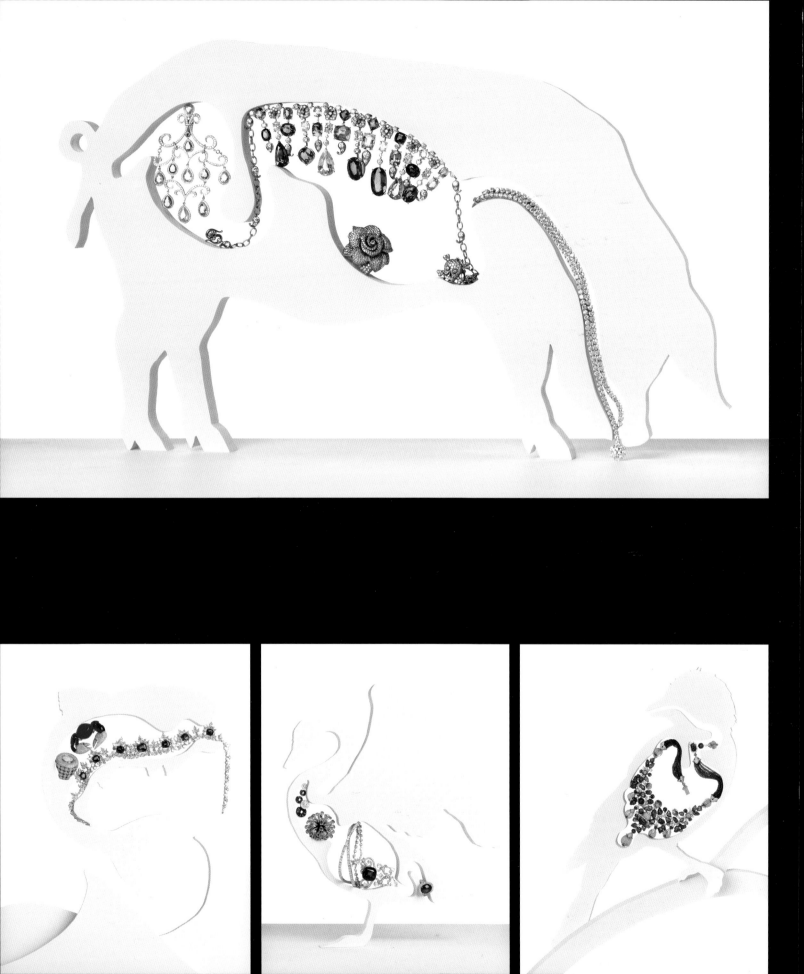

Tibo

Molly

1

2

3

4

festival for fashion, music & photography

www.6festival.at sented by Unit F bü... de

16-25
6/2006

GÜNTER EDER, ROMAN BREIER/
GRAFISCHES BÜRO
06-Festival for Fashion,
Music & Photography

**festival for fashion,
music &
photography**

warsztaty serigrafia
IPUS výtvarná umění
12. 12. – 14. 12. 2006
ostrava

DRUKUJ
I
MILCZ

WARSZTATY SERIGRAFIA

IPUS výtvarná umění

12. 12. – 14. 12. 2006

Ostrava

CLÉMENT GALLET
Evolution

SPACE AND TIME

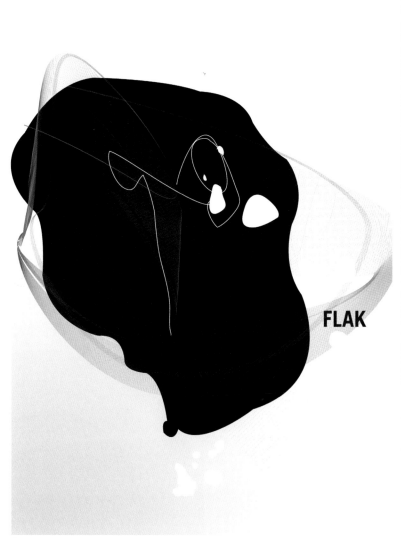

FLAK

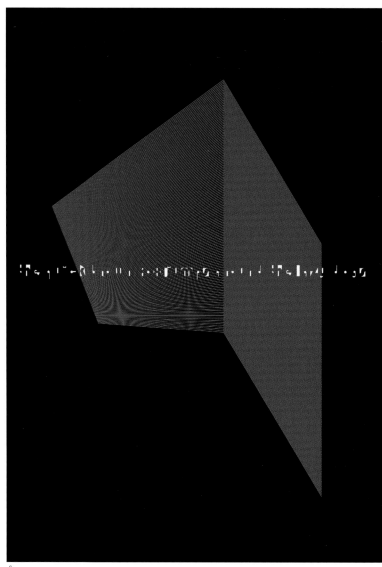

SARA HARAIGUE
[1] _Flak_
[2] _Build_

Page 180
Space & Time

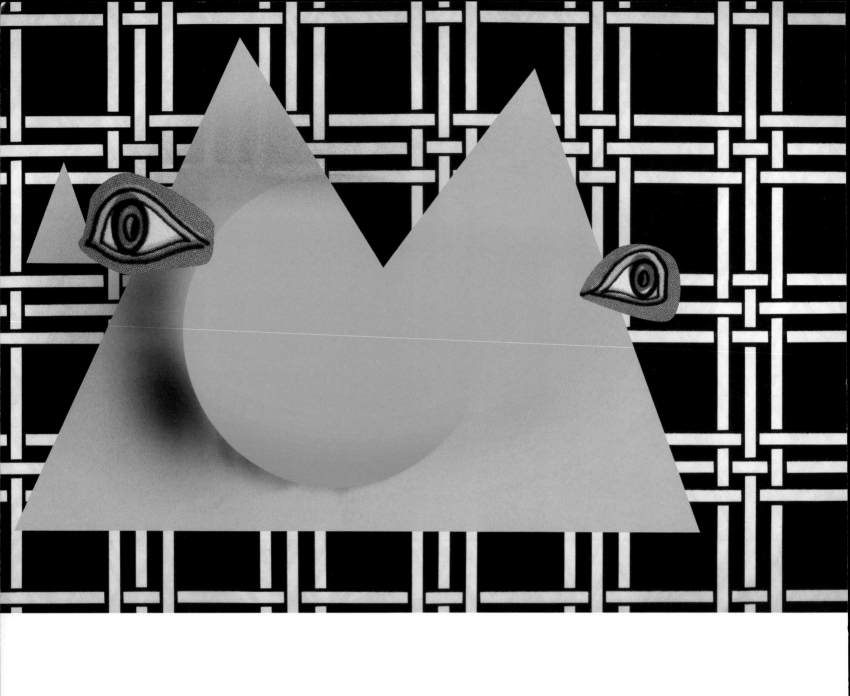

'66

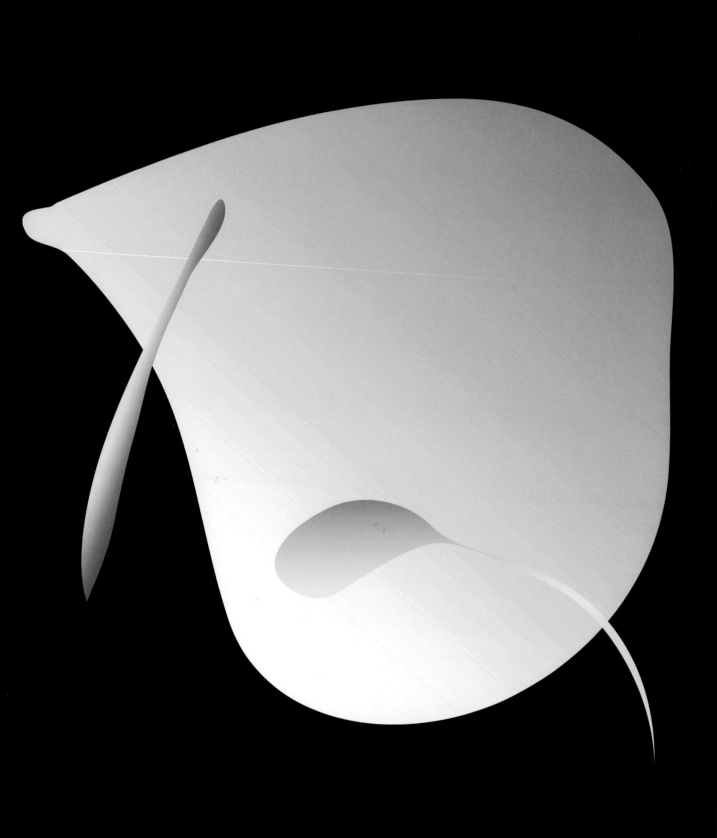

UNTITLED 2

Ny kantine 4/9-06. Brug den til udstillingsrum, fredagsbar, filmaften mm...

Ny kantine 4/9-06. Brug den til udstillingsrum, fredagsbar, filmaften mm...

MEJDEJ
Brug Din Kantine/
Use Your Canteen

Ny kantine 4/9-06. Brug den til udstillingsrum, fredagsbar, filmaften mm...

Booka Shade

Planetary
City Tales

HORT
Booka Shade
(album/single artwork)

«The season to be jolly» «The most wonderful time of the year» «All I want for Christmas is you» «Driving home for Christmas» «Walking in a Winter Wonderland»

Many artists sang about the Holiday Season. The time of the year in which all seems to be magnificent and full of joy. Nevertheless many of us experience the huge tension and feel very desolate for various reasons.

We undertake quite a lot during the Holiday Season. This time

The answers: 50% «Yes, usually» 34% «Sometimes» 14% «No, never» 373 people in the test declare they usually feel lonely during the Holiday Season. The poll learns the most wonderful time of the year isn't that much of a glorious period for many of us.

If it seems like there is no one to turn to in the atmosphere of family and friends, maybe it is best to consider volunteering to help those less fortunate. Life Coach Elizabeth Scott about helping the poor: «Many people report

causes many of us to spend more time indoors, many people are affected to some degree by a type of depression known as Seasonal Affective Disorder. It's a subtle, but very real condition that can cast a pall over the whole season and be a source of stress and unhappiness during a time that people expect to feel just the opposite.»

Problems won't disappear just because it is Christmas. TV Coach Liz Tucker advises: «Take positive steps to bring pleasure and satisfaction into your

dealing with consequences (debt, weight gain, memories of embarrassing behaviour) that can linger long after the season is over.» But what about some tips to have a healthy Christmas? Just like every other day at the year, a good breakfast is very important. A good breakfast does not create the feeling of longing for a food hurricane during the rest of the day. Well-loved Nutritionist Fiona Hunter adds: «For the main meal keep the starter light and simple — it means less work for whoever's doing the

body.» It is also indescribably important to keep on giving our bodies the exact amount of fresh oxygen we need. We are like Christmas trees and need to breathe, especially during the Holiday Season.

3
Avoid choking boredom

Some of us endure during never ending Christmas suppers from suffocating tiresomeness. Things slightly change only when desert — and the end of all the suffering — comes nearby. We feel we need to cut down tremendously on so called togetherness. Personal Growth Teacher Elizabeth Scott advices. «With family and friends, it's important to be aware of your limitations. Think back to previous years and try to pinpoint how much togetherness you and your family can take before feeling negative stress. Can you limit the number of parties you attend or throw, or the time you spend at each? Can you limit your time with family to a smaller timeframe that will still feel special and joyous, without draining you?»

Innocent Tension Fighter Michael Gutteridge suggests mental backup: Another important factor in being able to resist or cope with stress is to have some kind of social support mechanism – both in practical terms (someone to do things for you) and emotional terms (a non-judgmental shoulder to cry on if necessary but definitely someone to talk to).»

Lovely well-informed Christmas Survivor Liz Tucker: «Remember that Christmas day is just one day. So if you have commitments that you have to honour on that day, create your own perfect day on another date in the holiday period — book a pampery day at a spa, or disappear off to the seaside with your loved ones.»

4
Less work, less stress

We all want to be the best host, the best son, daughter or parent during the Holiday Season. Therefore, much needs to be done. Sending sweet cards and posh invitations, arranging flowers, baking exquisite pies, making delicious puddings, seeing old friends, and gardening. We often end up exhausted in the end of all the running. Often a lack of accurate scheduling is guilty of all miseries. In most occasions all activities could have been planned easily on a smaller scale.

Another great advice comes from amazing Wellbeing Instructor Elizabeth Scott. «Send cards, for example, but only to those with whom you maintain regular communication. Or, don't include a personal note or letter in each one. Find a way to simplify. The same goes for the baking — will anyone be enraged if you buy baked goods from the bakery instead? If you find ways to cut corners or tone down the activities that are important to you and your family, you may enjoy them much more.»

To kill all the stress, well known Guide to Housekeeping Sarah Aguirre suggests to make a special planner to schedule all activities during the Holiday Season: «The Holiday Season inevitably brings a ton of stress and confusion. There is so much to coordinate, organize, and prepare. Couple these challenges with the desire to have everything perfect, and you've got a recipe for emotional disaster. This year take some of the stress away from the season by organizing your own Holiday Planning Notebook. Use the notebook to hold and organize all of your holiday lists, travel reservations, receipts for gifts, gift lists, recipes, etc. They will all be in one place and ready to go when you need them.»

5
In the end: Deal with it

There is no way to escape the Holiday Season. The best thing to suggest, is the one to cope with it. All the stress and those sudden pains showing up already at the end of September can be restricted best with humour, Stress Expert Michael Gutteridge says: «Having a positive mental attitude and a sense of humour is really important for your well-being. Be positive rather than dwelling on the negatives in life. Don't focus on the things that can go wrong but on the things you will enjoy. Give yourself some credit for what you do well and remember the nice things that happened last year and see if you can laugh about the things that didn't go quite to plan.» Face it. Life Expert Liz Tucker: «Christmas is not compulsory, but so many people start complaining about it months in advance as if it is some sort of endurance test! Christmas is supposed to be a pleasurable time, and if you start off with a negative attitude, you can guarantee that it will be a very negative event.»

Don't let negativity get into your Holiday Season too much. Always keep in mind there's a happy ending to every story. In the end, it worked out perfectly well for George Michael aswell: «A face on a lover with a fire in his heart. A man under cover but you tore me apart. Now I've found a real love you'll never fool me again.» Don't let them fool you and enjoy the most wonderful time of the year! •

All great advice and even more can be read on the web. Visit stress.about.com for Elizabeth Scott. Visit housekeeping.about.com for Sarah Aguirre. Visit survivingchristmas.co.uk for Michael Gutteridge and Liz Tucker

Story and graphic design: Rob Giesendorf

«Last Christmas I gave you my heart, but the very next day you gave it away.»

Life during the Holiday Season

of the year involves a large sequence of social activities including pleasant parties and affairs, holiday shopping, the exchange of presents and the mailing of cheerful Christmas cards. No wonder this season in particular can cause a large amount of all kinds of unpleasant irregularities.

1
Feelings of «No one to turn to — All on my own»

Those ones who already feel lonely during the year, will feel worse during the Christmas period. The season has without a doubt a way of placing already enormous feelings of solitude and misery under a microscope, and magnifying them easily times 100.

734 individuals answered following question «Do you feel lonely during the Holiday Season?» in a poll on the website of keen Stress Teacher Elizabeth Scott. The results are incredibly horrific.

these experiences to be extremely fulfilling, and your focus will be on what you have rather than what you lack.»

Loneliness during the Holiday Season is also closely connected to the loss of dear ones. Maybe because our beloved ones are deceased — maybe because our relationships have come to an end. «Last Christmas I gave you my heart, but the very next day you gave it away,» Wham! sang during the 1980s. One needs to be very strong to cope with painful romantic memories and conflicts «This year, to save me from tears, I'll give it to someone special.»

If you think you are the only one dealing with loneliness, you are wrong. Well-sproken Stress Guide Elizabeth Scott about Seasonal Affective Disorder (SAD): «An often unrecognized problem that comes with the holiday season is actually a by-product of the seasons changing from fall to winter. As daylight diminishes and the weather

life over the Holiday Period and put your problems on hold. Say to yourself that you are going to do everything that you can to make Christmas as enjoyable as possible, and this will involve addressing negative aspects that could prevent that from happening.»

2
Do face boundries

We attempt to lose ourselves completely during the Holiday Season. There are no boundaries when it comes to snacking and drinking loads. According to the faulty habits of being beside ourselves when it comes to eating, spending and taking several walks on several wild sides, Inspired Stress Manager Elizabeth Scott says: «An overabundance of parties and gift-giving occasions lead many people to eat, drink, and be merry — often to excess. The temptation to overindulge in spending, rich desserts or alcohol can cause many people

cooking and less calories and fat. Choosing a stuffing made from chestnuts or dried fruits instead of the traditional sausage meat stuffing and you'll also save about 100 calories and 11g fat per serving. Bigger is always better particularly when you're talking about roast potatoes. Larger potatoes absorb less fat during roasting. Par boil potatoes first, then brush with a little olive oil before finishing off in the oven.»

But if all of it didn't work out properly, here are some tips to give the hangover the heavy ho-ho by Hangover Coach Fiona Hunter: «Restorative brew. No, not lager: the caffeine in tea or coffee will give you a kick-start while rehydrating your system. Try a large glass of apple juice, sweetened with a little honey, topped up with a little sparkling water. It's gentler on the stomach than orange juice and provides an instant hit of glucose which will help restore blood sugar levels, vitamin C and fluid to rehydrate the

Sikkens Foundation stimulates those social, cultural and scientific developments in society where color plays a specific role. This is primarily done by awarding the Sikkens Prize and organizing the Piet Mondrian Lecture.

The Sikkens Prize, a crystal prism symbolising the phenomenon of color, was inaugurated in 1959 and presented to the Dutch architect Gerrit Rietveld. Followed by Le Corbusier, Theo van Doesburg and Donald Judd amongst others…

With the establishment in 1979 of the Piet Mondrian Lecture, Sikkens Foundation has been able to contribute to the debate about the cultural meaning of color, through lectures by Rem Koolhaas, Simon Schama, Nancy Troy and Umberto Eco.

Its immediate aim is to bring about inspiring confrontations between Dutch cultural life and domestic and foreign scientific practitioners and artists.

SikkensFoundation

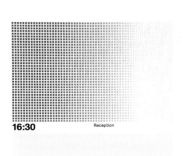

Joe Zucker

The Good, the Bad and the Ugly

ScheiblerMitte

Pegman, 1992
Acryl, Holz, Pressspan / acrylic, pegboard, plywood
244 x 124 cm / 96 x 48.8 in.

Rocky Marciano vs Ezzard Charles, Tough Guys, 1976
Acryl, Baumwolle auf Rhoplex auf Leinwand /
acrylic, cotton on rhoplex on canvas
2-teilig, 460 x 190 cm / two parts, 181 x 74.8 in.
Sammlung Lilja Art Fund Foundation

Black Volcano, 2005
Acryl auf Leinwand und Holz / acrylic on canvas and wood
Diptychon / diptych
A: 118 x 240 cm / 46.50 x 94.50 in. / B: 114 x 236 cm / 45 x 92 in.
Museum Ludwig Köln

Joe Zucker
The Good, the Bad and the Ugly
19. Januar - 8. März 2008
Artist Talk: Joe Zucker mit Mark Gisbourne,
Samstag, 19. Januar 2008, 18 Uhr,
mit anschliessender Eröffnung 19-21 Uhr

The Good, the Bad and the Ugly ist eine Auswahl
monumentaler Bilder des amerikanischen Künstlers
Joe Zucker (geb. 1941 in Chicago). Die Werke stam-
men aus den Jahren 1973 bis 2007. Zuckers erste
Einzelausstellung in Berlin bietet eine subjektive Sicht
auf die große Vielfalt der von Zucker erforschten
Stilmittel. Eine Klammer um diese vielfältige und
experimentierfreudige Produktion bilden Zuckers hoch
entwickeltes Formverständnis, sein Bewusstsein für
Geschichte und seine scharfe Ironie.

„Joe Zucker gehört seit mehr als 40 Jahren zu den
innovativsten Künstlern Amerikas. Seine Malerei ist
persönlich, verschroben, eigenwillig und oft rätselhaft.
Sein Stil leitet sich von Arbeitsprozessen ab – manche
davon einfach, andere bemerkenswert komplex. Auch
die Bildinhalte stehen zumeist in irgendeinem Zusam-
menhang mit den jeweiligen Materialien und Arbeits-
weisen. So hat Zucker Bilder von Baumwollplantagen
mit farbgetränkten Wattebäuschen gemalt.
Einige seiner Arbeiten enthalten nicht nur die an der
Entstehung beteiligten Werkzeuge, sondern verdeutli-
chen auch deren Anwendung als Teil der Darstellung.
Zucker hat außerdem Bilder erzeugt, in denen die
Farbe nicht auf eine Leinwand oder einen sonstigen
Untergrund aufgetragen ist, sondern buchstäblich im
Raum schwebt, so dass das Medium Farbe nur sich
selbst darstellt und nichts sonst. Beim Gießen, Kneten
und sonstigen Manipulieren der Farbe entstanden sehr
persönliche Arbeiten, zu denen man sich unmöglich
einen anderen Urheber als Joe Zucker denken kann.
Diese Werke sind geradezu der Inbegriff eigenständi-
ger Erfindung."
Betsy Sussler in "Joe Zucker by Chuck Close", BOMB Magazine, Nr. 100,
Sommer 2007.

Ein Künstlergespräch zwischen Joe Zucker und dem
Kunstkritiker Mark Gisbourne findet um 18 Uhr am Tag
der Eröffnung statt.

The Good, the Bad and the Ugly is a selection of monu-
mental paintings by the American artist Joe Zucker
(*1941 Chicago) from the years 1973 until 2007. His first
solo show in Berlin offers a subjective view onto the
myriad of styles the artist has explored. This highly
diverse and experimental output is unified by a keen
formal and historical sensibility and devastating wit.

"Joe Zucker has consistently for over four decades
been one of America's most innovative artists.
His paintings are personal, quirky, idiosyncratic, and
often puzzling. His style is rooted in processes, some
simple, others remarkably complex. His imagery most
often relates in some way to the materials and processes (for example, cotton plantation imagery executed in
cotton balls rolled in paint). He has made paintings that
include the tools that made them integrated into the
works themselves and illustrate the use of those tools
as part of the imagery. He has made paintings in which
the paint is not applied to canvas or any other ground,
but literally floats in space – the medium purely being
itself. Pouring, squeezing and manipulating paint, he
fashions paintings so personal it would be impossible to
imagine anyone else having made them. This is the
definition of personal invention."
Betsy Sussler, from "Joe Zucker by Chuck Close," BOMB Magazine, issue #100,
Summer 2007

An artist talk with Joe Zucker and the art critic
Mark Gisbourne will take place at 6:00 pm on the day
of the opening.

Charlottenstrasse 2
10969 Berlin
office@aurelscheibler.com
T. +49 (0)30 25 93 86 07
F. +49 (0)30 25 93 86 08

Öffnungszeiten:
Mittwoch – Samstag 11-18 Uhr
und nach Vereinbarung

ScheiblerMitte

KOLEKTIV
Majáles Poster

NARN CONFERENCE 2007

Mutual partnerships shaping
the future of universities.

KAZUMASA NAGAIN TYÖPÖYTÄ

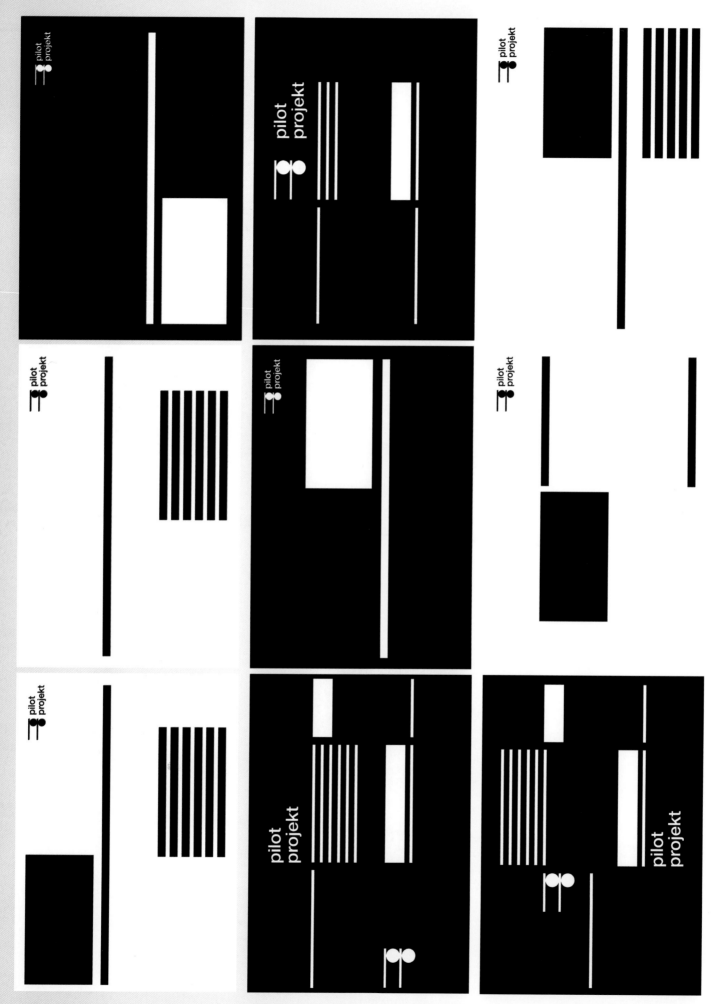

The "Amen Break" is a drum solo performed by G.C. Coleman. It is 5.20 seconds long and consists of 4 bars from the 1969 song "Amen, Brother" by The Winstons. It is one of the first drum loops to be sampled, and has become one of the most sampled break beats in history.

http://en.wikipedia.org/wiki/Amen_break
http://nktrcradio.com/pages/amen_mp4.html

In the long term we are all dead

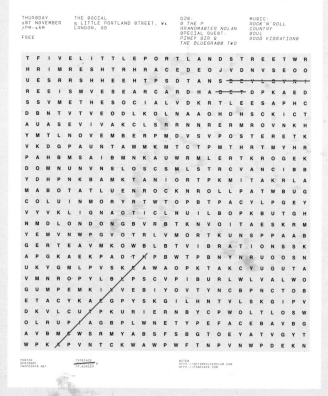

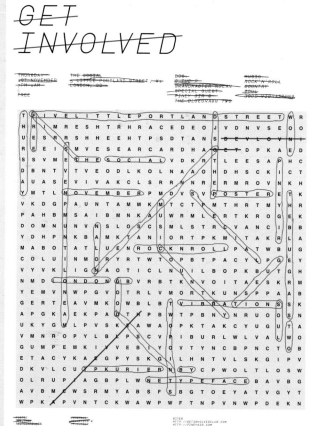

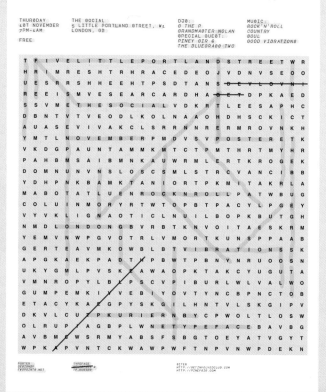

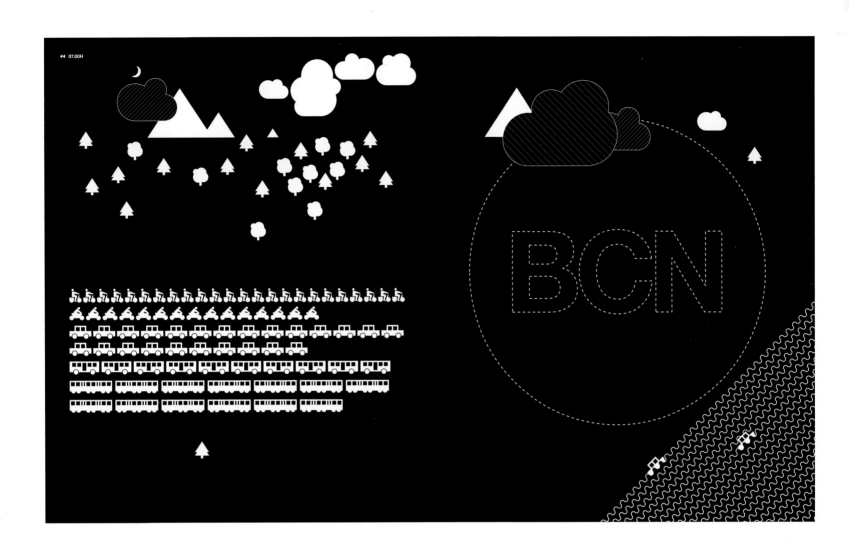

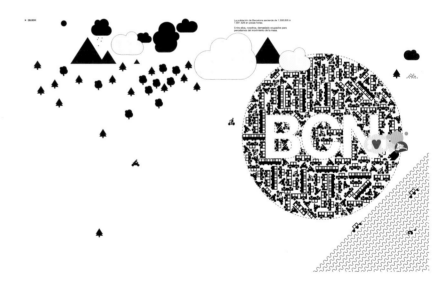

Impulsem k napsání článku byl rozhovor s Vladimírem Körnerem otištěný v Tvaru 19. 10 2006 pod názvem. Poláci jsou absolutní špička a velmi kulturní národ, podobně jako třeba Slováci nebo Maďaři - na rozdíl od Čechů. Češi jsou na rozdíl od Slováků nebo Poláků dost nekulturní. Své světce zabíjejí, špičky jsou pryč a elita není. Toto vyhrocené srovnání mě poněkud vyvedlo z rovnováhy. Jestliže měl Vladimír Körner potřebu uvést jej dokonce dvakrát, nepůjde zřejmě o pouhé uřeknutí. Vzal jsem vážně stylizaci, která se kolem něj trochu vytváří, stylizaci vidoucího mezi slepými a začal o jeho slovech přemýšlet. Sám přece, jak naznačil v jiném, starším interview pro MF Dnes, myšlení u lidí trochu postrádá.

REPUBLIC

STRANA 4

STRANA 5

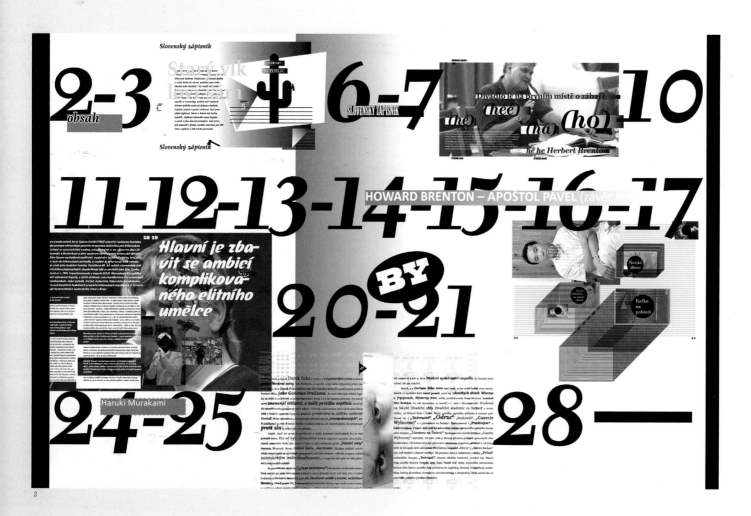

Divadlo je na prvním místě o zábavě (he) (hee) (ha) (ho) he he Herbert Brenton

HOWARD BRENTON – APOŠTOL PAVEL (závěr ...)

Hlavní je zbavit se ambicí komplikovaného elitního umělce

Haruki Murakami

Norské dřevo

Kafka na pobřeží

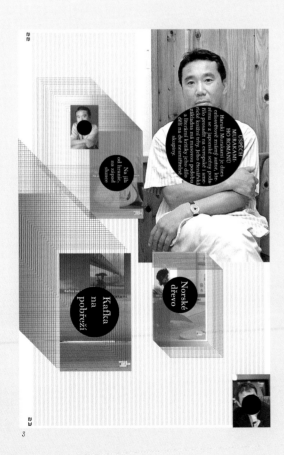

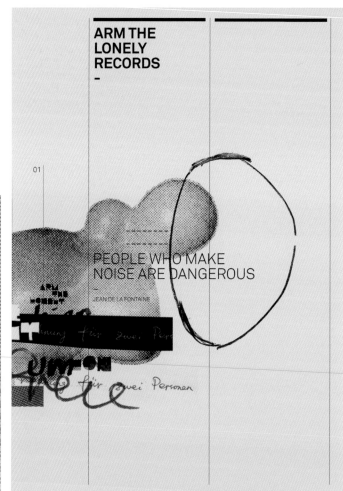

ARM THE LONELY RECORDS

—

01

PEOPLE WHO MAKE NOISE ARE DANGEROUS

—
JEAN DE LA FONTAINE

ARM THE LONELY RECORDS

—

04

ROOMS AND PLACES

Music necessarily happens in a defined timeframe. Arm the Lonely is also trying to locate the music in a specific space. Trying out music in different places is a criterion to find personal, specific, subjective access. Music anchors in a room and spreads out, melts away, changes according to room situations in which music occurs. Some songs sound best in a second floor flat in the evening with the windows open onto the street, mixing up with the sounds of the city which is slowly getting tired of a hard working day.

Some songs need a close listening situation together with a person you adore, some a tense concert situation with sweaty bodies, some open car windows in the summer sun, some maybe a dark sleeping room and the noises of your neighbour having sex with his new girlfriend coming through the wall and others profit from dogs barking or the voices of children playing in the park, with the ornamental decoration in a viennese café or the white walls of my own living room.

ALEXANDER EGGER
Drowning in a Sea
of Possibilities

Page 206
Arm the Lonely
(A quotation by Savoy Grand)

MUSEUM PAPER

shoot • draw • write

ISSUE FOUR

Fernando Elvira • French • IHOC • Stefan Marx
Rick Myers • Patrick O'Dell • Josh Petherick • Deanna Templeton

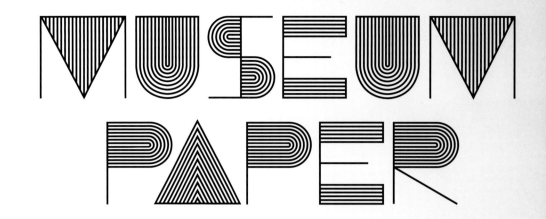

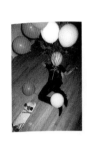

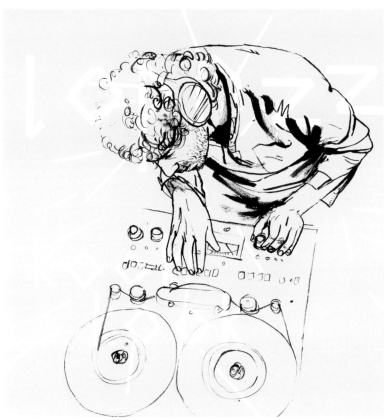

HORT
Lopazz
(album/single artwork)

WELCOMETO.AS
Program Théâtre
de Vevey 2007–2008

Page 212
KOLEKTIV
Majáles Poster

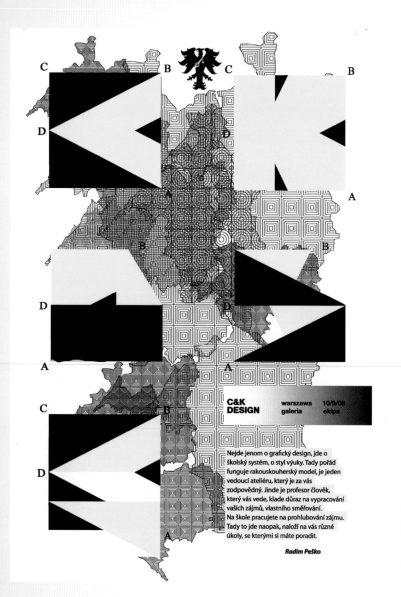

C&K
DESIGN   warszawa   10/9/08
          galeria   ekipa

Nejde jenom o grafický design, jde o
školský systém, o styl výuky. Tady pořád
funguje rakouskouherský model, je jeden
vedoucí ateliéru, který je za vás
zodpovědný. Jinde je profesor člověk,
který vás vede, klade důraz na vypracování
vašich zájmů, vlastního směřování.
Na škole pracujete na prohlubování zájmu.
Tady to jde naopak, naloží na vás různé
úkoly, se kterými si máte poradit.

Radim Peško

Today I am a C&K soldier
and my future is unsure

C&K
DESIGN   warszawa
          galeria

KOLEKTIV
Ck Exhibition

Page 215
*The Summer Film School
in Uherské Hradište
2008/Posters & Stickers*

214

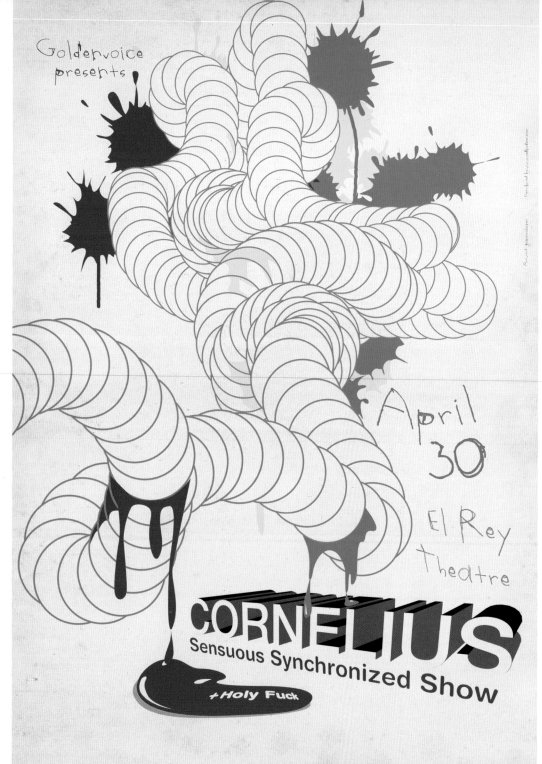

1

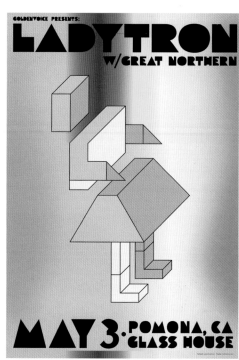

2

3

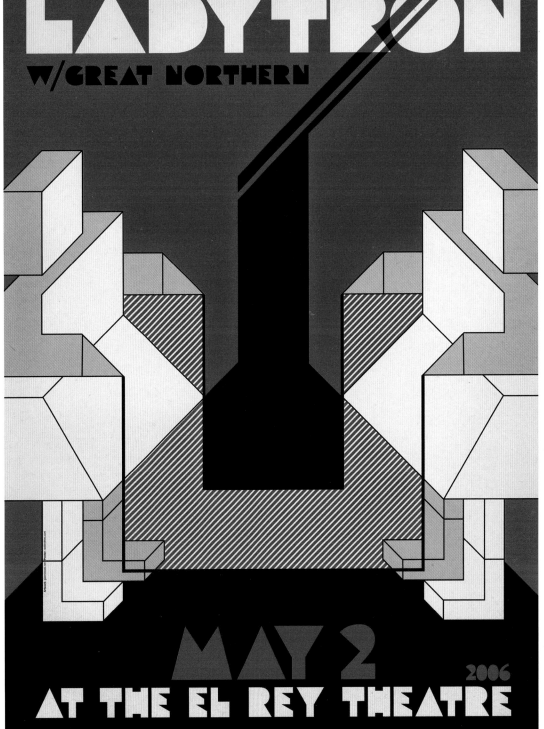

WELCOMETO.AS
Chronicle Books Design
Fellowship Poster

Page 219
WELCOMETO.AS &
RADIM PESKO
Cool School Exhibition

FIVE DESIGN FELLOWSHIPS
WINTER–SPRING 2007

ADULT TRADE:
BEAUTIFUL BOOKS ON A VARIETY
OF INTERESTING SUBJECTS

CHILDREN'S:
CREATIVE, FUN AND EDUCATIONAL
BOOKS FOR CHILDREN

GIFT:
EXCITING KITS, DECKS, CALENDARS,
CARDS AND OTHER GIFT ITEMS

INDUSTRIAL / PRODUCT DESIGN:
INNOVATIVE PRODUCTS AND
PACKAGING DESIGN

MARKETING DESIGN:
DYNAMIC PROMOTIONAL
MATERIALS FOR ALL
DIVISIONS

www.chroniclebooks.com/designfellowship

PORTFOLIO DUE:
NOVEMBER 7, 2006

START DATE:
JANUARY 3, 2007
END DATE:
JUNE 29, 2007

CHRONICLE BOOKS
85 SECOND STREET,
6TH FLOOR
SAN FRANCISCO,
CALIFORNIA 94105

Design by Adam Macháček, Printed by Bloom Screen Printing Co, Oakland, CA

Cool School
Fresh Graphic Design from Switzerland
and Holland

The exhibition opening and lecture by the
project authors Adam Machacek & Radim Peško
will take place on Tuesday,
October 20 at 6 p.m.

21. 9. – 2. 10. 2005

galeria architektury SARP
ul. Dyrekcyjna 9, 40-013 Katowice
tel 032 25 39 774
fax 032 25 39 230
galeria@sarp.katowice.pl

partners: DIE GESTALTEN VERLAG, JRP RINGIER, RINGIER PRINT, printed at AAAD, Prague, by Antonín Kornátek and René Řebec

With the kind support of PRO HELVETIA,
Arts Council of Switzerland

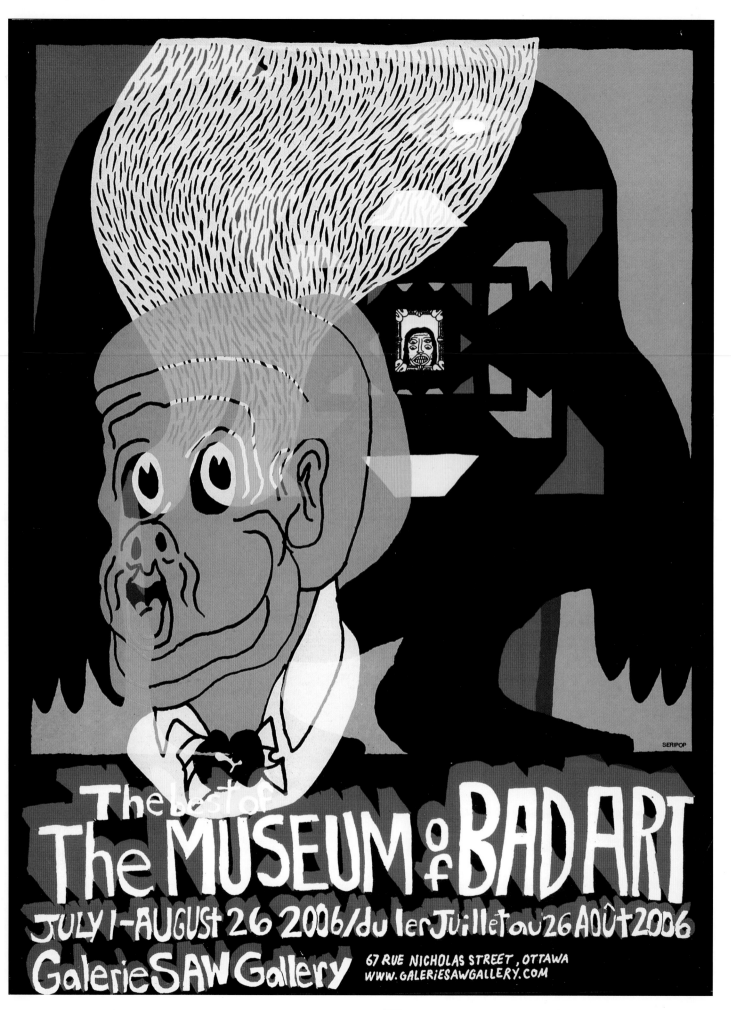

1

2

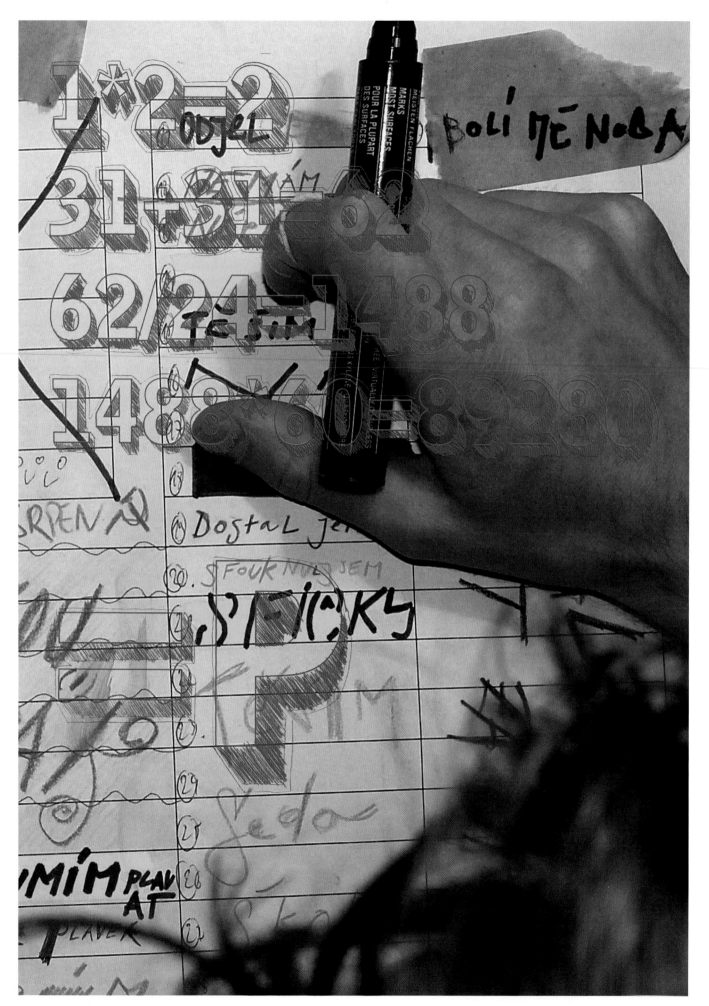

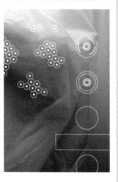

ISBN: 80-7027-143-4

INTERNATIONAL ISSUE
GERMAN / ENGLISH

novum plus

EDUCATION

NGDESIGN
ELEGANZ & POWER
ITALIAN STYLE

TWOPOINTS.NET
IN DER WELT ZU HAUSE
CITIZENS OF THE WORLD

**STOCKHOLM
DESIGN LAB**
GANZHEITLICHE LÖSUNGEN
INTEGRATED SOLUTIONS

4 198092 909809   10

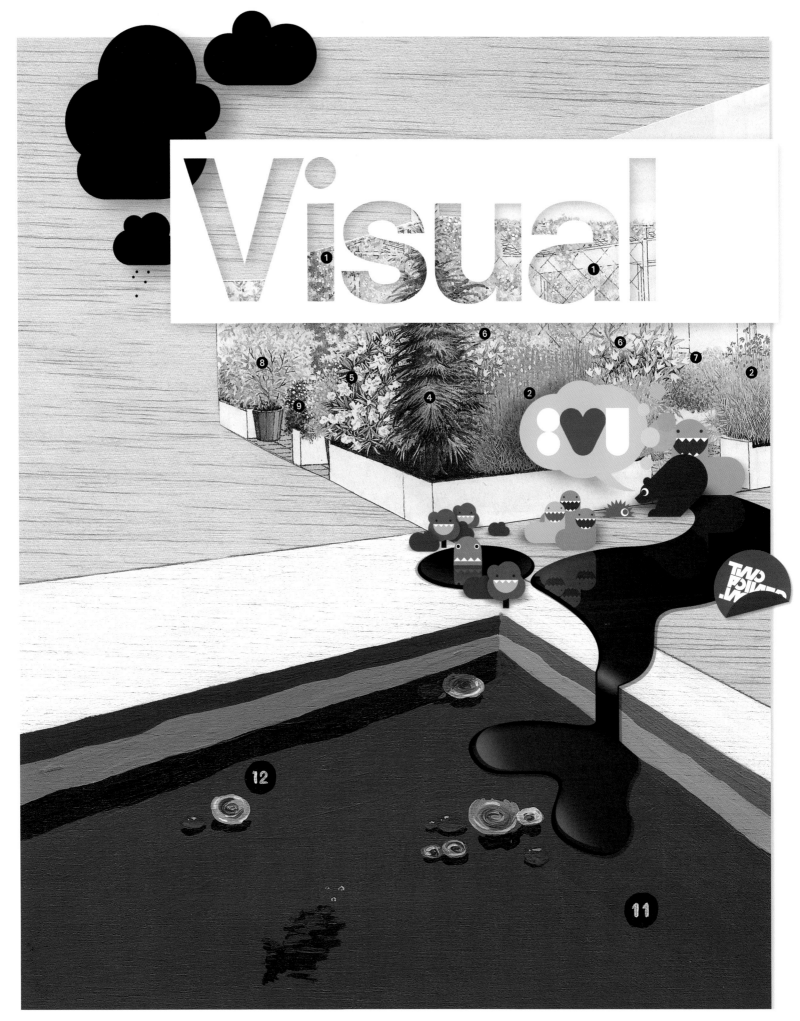

LILI FLEURY
1 _Borderline_
2 _Nothing Else Matters_
3 _Get Back_

Page 230
June

1

2

3

HELENE BUILLY
*Scène Nationale
de Dieppe*

SAISON **05-06**
Saison sourires aux lèvres
cirque, théâtre, danse, musique, cinéma ...

D S N
Dieppe
Scène
Nationale

www.dsn.asso.fr
02 35 82 04 43

HELENE BUILLY
The Cloud Making
Machine

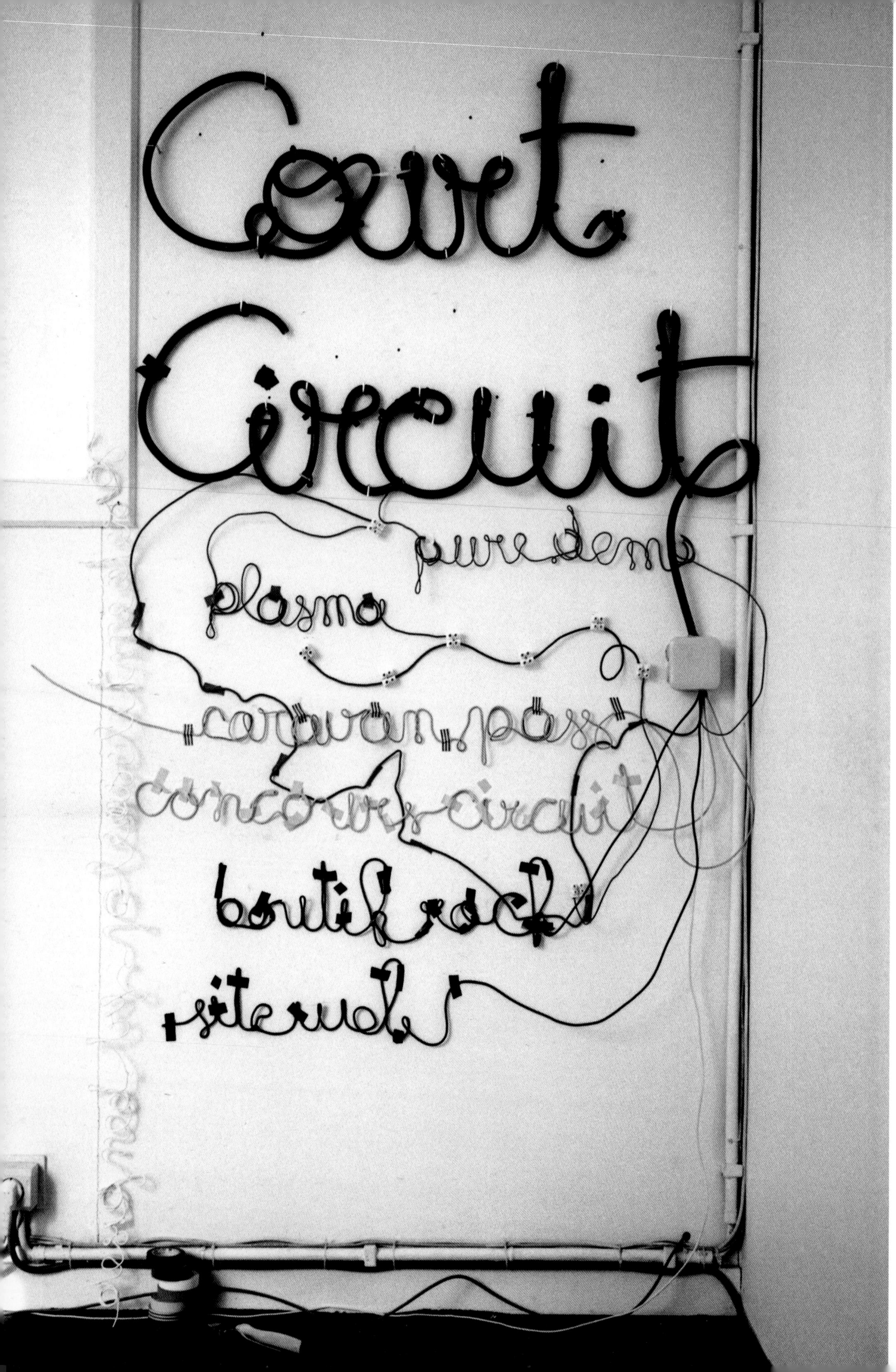

PLEASELETMEDESIGN
Court Circuit

The Experimental
Tropic Blues Band

1. Rene The Renegade
2. Jealous Rock
3. Rising From The Dead
4. The Gambler
5. Twice Blues
6. Voodoo Rise
7. Gangrena Blues
8. Garbage Man
9. Snake Spirit
10. Dry Whiskey
11. Hallelujah
12. Mexico Green Blues
13. I Went Down
14. Evil Got The Bone

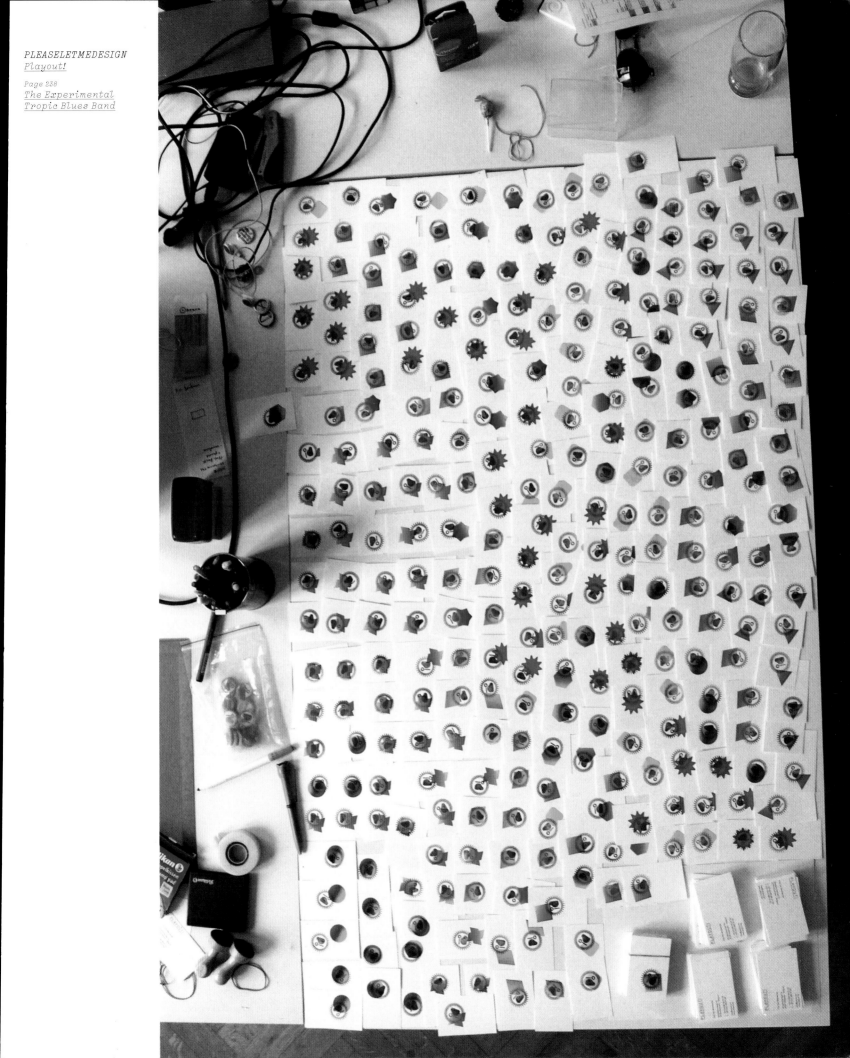

PIXELGARTEN
Untitled

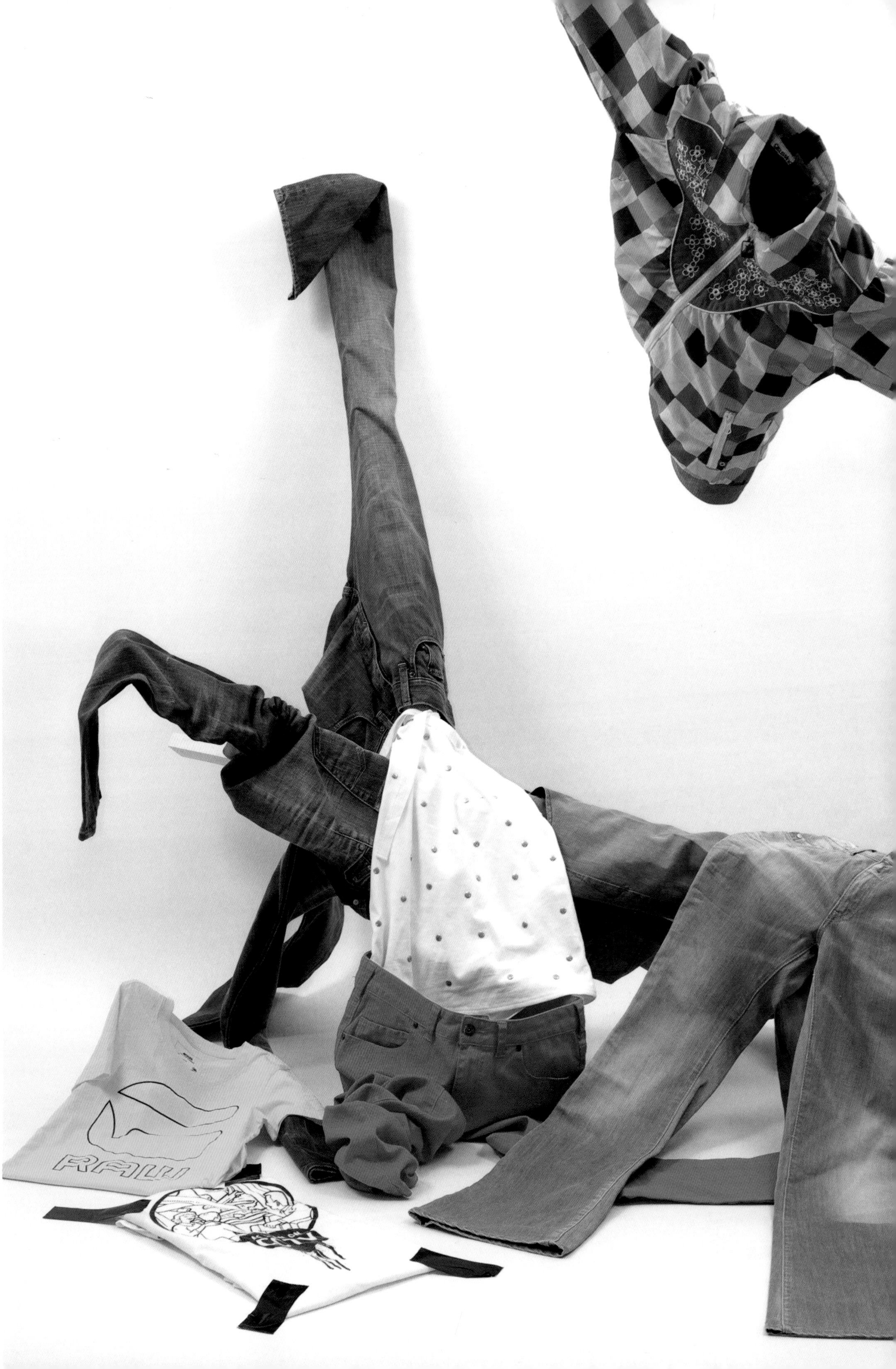

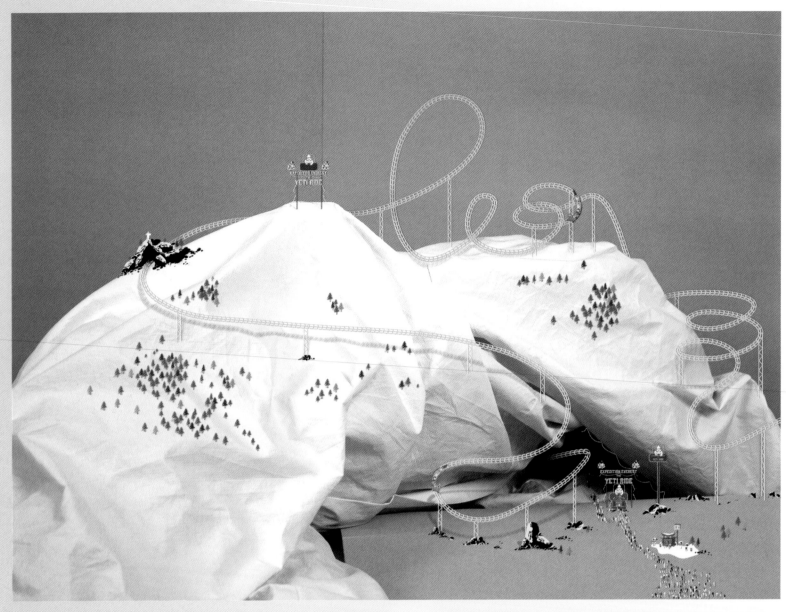

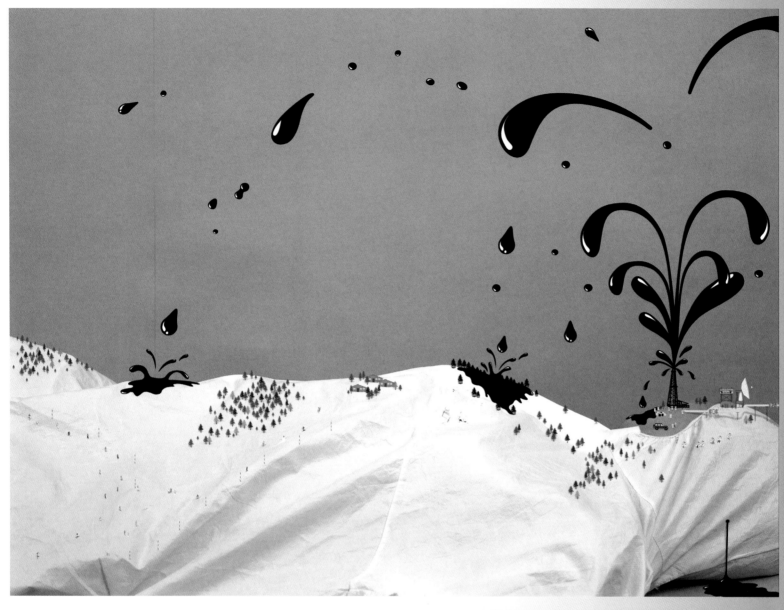

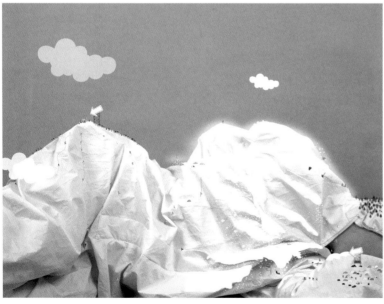

PIXELGARTEN
Höhenluft

SHOTOPOP
1 _Tooth Hip_
2 _Tubguy_
3 _Lost!_

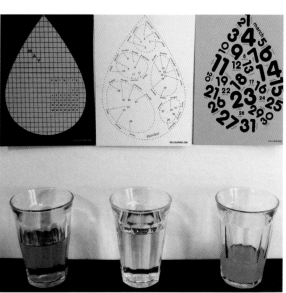

PANDAROSA
[1] *Various Titles*
[2] *Miss Pink & Miss Saigon*

MUSEUM STUDIO
Breakfast Club

Page 251
LULA
[1-2] *Come On*
[3] *Strössel*

1

2

3

PIXELGARTEN
Scout Uniform

Page 252
JULIEN VALLÉE

2–3 _Quebec Annual Graphic_
Design Studios Guide 2008

Every Morning, I check Manystuff

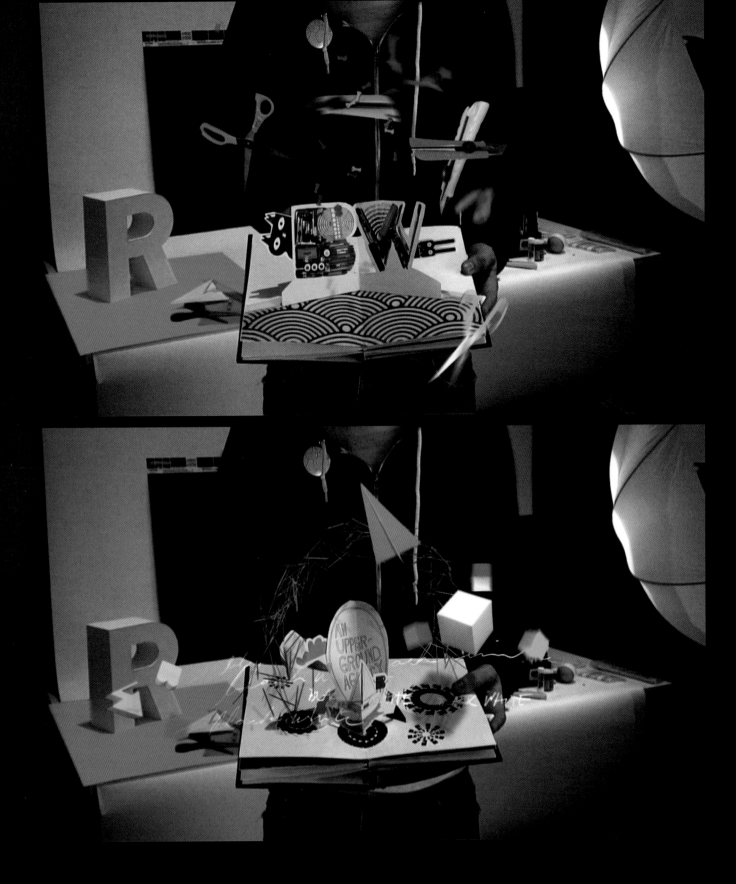

JULIEN VALLÉE
Black & White Teaser

CONTAINERPLUS
Footwear Fairy Tales:
[1] Rapunzel
[2] Cinderella
[3] Little Red Riding Hood
[4] Alice in Wonderland

2

3

4

PHILIPPE JARRIGEON
[1] *Pieds de Poule/Iris*
[2] *Pieds de Poule/Mortitia*

Page 258
Bunny Bunny

Page 260-261
Erwin

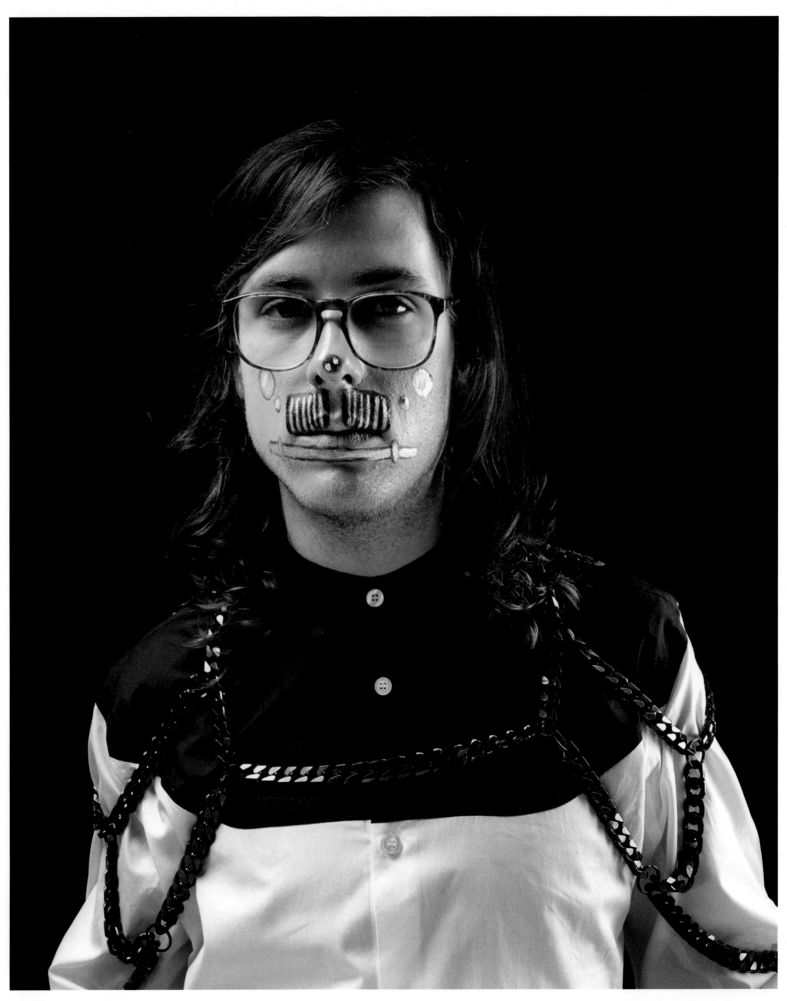

PIXELGARTEN
Dirk

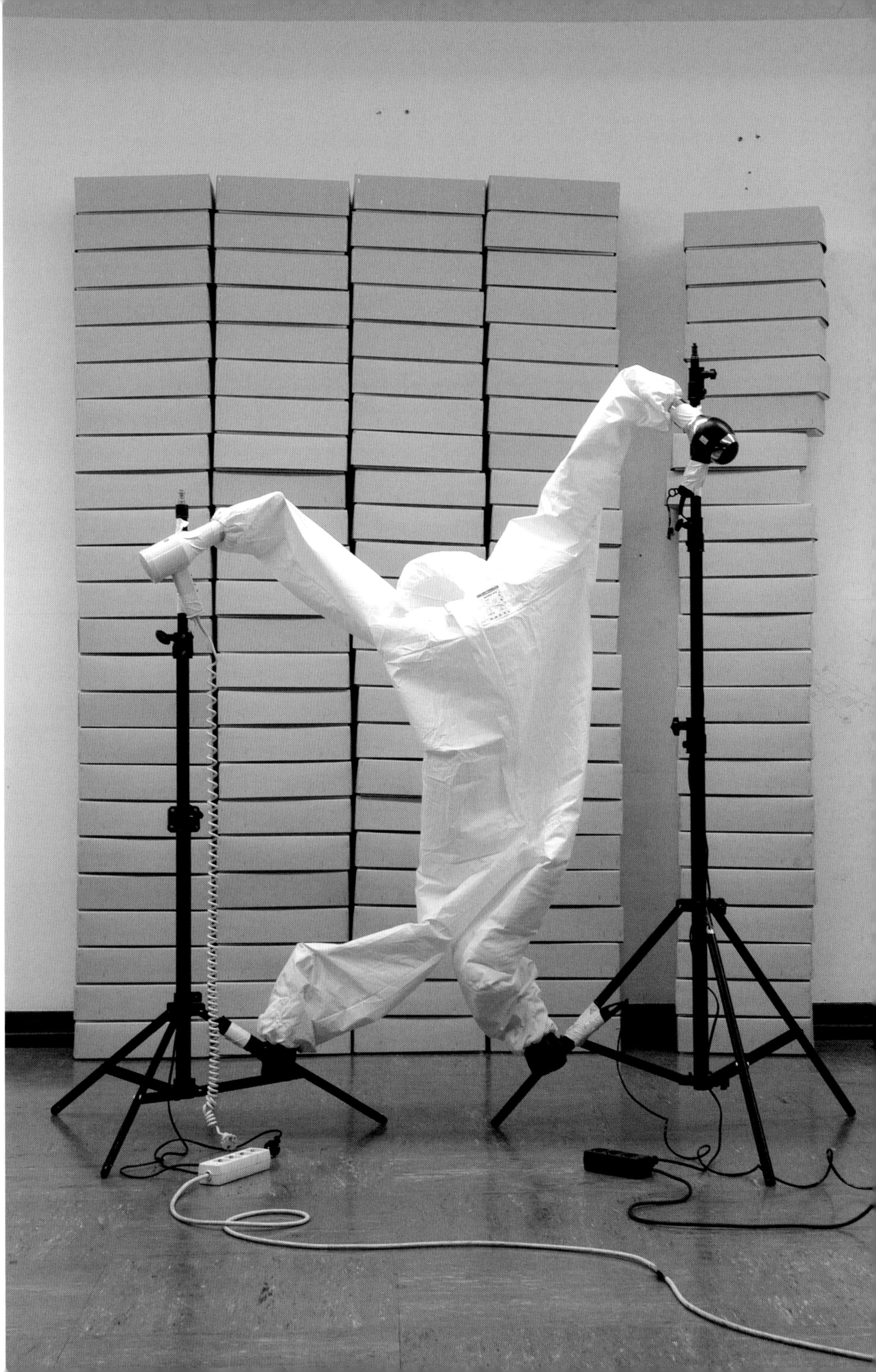

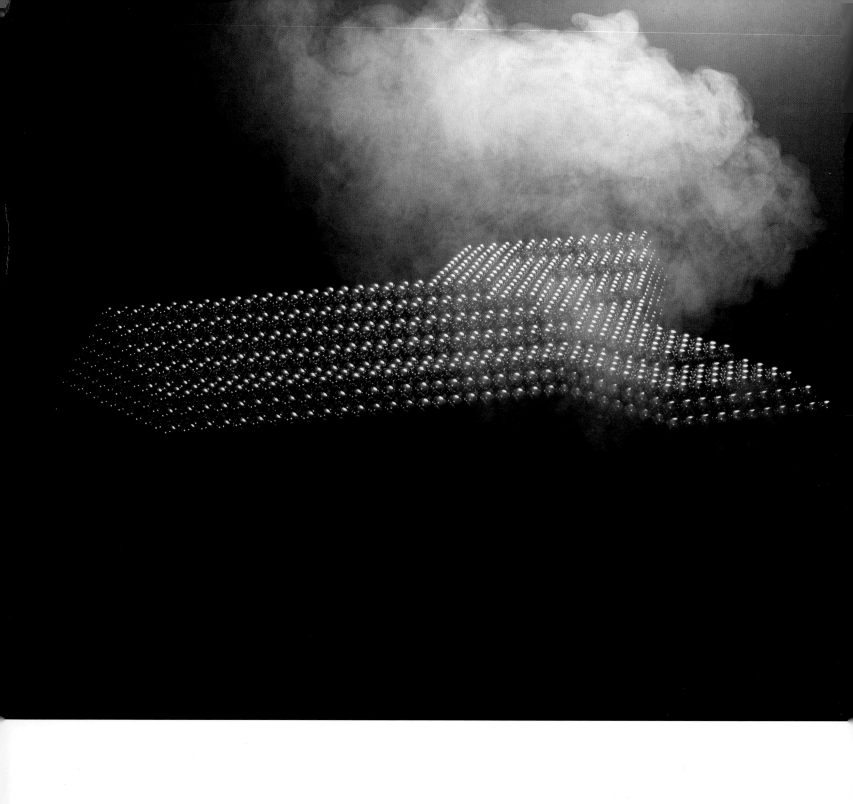

LEMON POPPY SEED
Multitasking Creativity

Edited by Robert Klanten, Hendrik Hellige, Adeline Mollard
Project management by Julian Sorge for Gestalten
Layout by Adeline Mollard for Gestalten
Cover by Théo Gènnitsakis/Paris Athens 24
Back Cover Hey by Théo Gènnitsakis/Paris Athens 24
Typeface: Lacrima by Alexander Meyer
Foundry: www.die-gestalten.de/fonts

Production management by Janni Milstrey for Gestalten
Printed by SIA Livonia Print, Riga
Made in Europe

Published by Gestalten, Berlin 2008

ISBN 978-3-89955-210-2